FOR THE DURATION

By kind permission of F. J. Mortimer, F.R.P.S., Editor of the "Amateur Photographer."   "THE GATE OF GOODBYE."

FOR THE DURATION
THE STORY OF THE THIRTEENTH
BATTALION THE RIFLE BRIGADE
BY D. H. ROWLANDS · WITH A FORE-
WORD BY CAPTAIN W. B. MAXWELL

The Naval & Military Press Ltd

Published by

The Naval & Military Press Ltd

Unit 5 Riverside, Brambleside
Bellbrook Industrial Estate
Uckfield, East Sussex
TN22 1QQ England

Tel: +44 (0)1825 749494

www.naval-military-press.com
www.nmarchive.com

Cover illustration: The Gate of Goodbye 1917
Francis James Mortimer, a prominent British Pictorialist, used his
darkroom skills to fuel England's patriotic fervour during World War I.
The Gate of Goodbye, his most popular and widely reproduced photograph,
depicts war-bound soldiers bidding farewell to their families at London's
Victoria Station. Although such scenes were common during the war years,
Mortimer's photograph is a composite, artfully assembled from more than
twenty different negatives—an ideologically motivated, aesthetically
perfected exaggeration of the truth.

In reprinting in facsimile from the original, any imperfections are inevitably reproduced
and the quality may fall short of modern type and cartographic standards.

DEDICATED
TO THE 768 GALLANT COMRADES
WHO PERISHED IN THE WAR
AND
TO THOSE OTHERS
WHO HAVE SINCE DIED

"They shall grow not old, as we that are left grow old.
Age shall not weary them, nor the years condemn.
At the going down of the sun and in the morning
We will remember them."

From "For the Fallen," by Laurence Binyon
Reprinted by permission

AUTHOR'S NOTE

THIS is a true story. It concerns the life of an Infantry Battalion whose members enlisted for the duration of the Great War. It is the chronicle of a Service Battalion of a famous Regiment, yet it may be that some of its pages tell the history, at least in part, of other units of the British Army during those eventful years 1914–1918.

The main theme is based on the official records of the 13th Battalion of The Rifle Brigade, and all the incidents described in the narrative really happened. The anecdotes and the personal impressions have been written from actual experience—some of it mine, some the experience of my Battalion friends—with the aid of private notes and a good memory.

It does not pretend to give a picture of the kind drawn by certain War films and novels, because there has been no attempt here to obtain effect at the expense of veracity, nor does it portray the life of the men in the trenches as one of brutality, profane language and licence.

Should the dates and names seem tedious to the general reader, I can only offer the excuse that they are naturally of great personal interest to the surviving members of the Battalion.

I acknowledge, gladly and gratefully, the kindness of the Committee of Imperial Defence (Military Branch), especially that of Mr. E. A. Dixon, and of the War Office Staff, including Mr. J. R.

Nelson, M.B.E., Mr. W. Y. Baldry, O.B.E., and my brother, Mr. A. Rowlands, M.B.E.—all of whom combined to give me access to the original War Diary and Part II Orders of the Battalion, and to assist me in many other ways. I wish also to thank War friends who have helped me to recall experiences, some humorous, some tragic, which we had together.

In addition I must express my gratitude to Mr. F. J. Mortimer, F.R.P.S., for the loan of his picture "The Gate of Goodbye," so memory-haunting and expressive, and to that distinguished author, Captain W. B. Maxwell, for his great kindness in providing the Foreword.

I have included the names of a few of my old comrades without seeking their permission, and I ask their indulgence. To all those great fellows I have omitted to mention, though deserving a place in this narrative, I tender my sincere apologies.

D. H. ROWLANDS

"Winscombe,"
Rhiwbina, Cardiff

CONTENTS

CHAP.		PAGE
	Author's Note	7
	Foreword	13
I.	Soldiers in the Making	19
II.	Early Days in France	32
III.	Gommecourt 1915	39
IV.	Le Gastineau—Auxi—and Back Again	54
V.	The Tragic Summer of 1916	66
VI.	The Battle of the Ancre	81
VII.	The Battle of Arras 1917	90
VIII.	The Ypres Salient	102
IX.	Still in the Salient	112
X.	Old Haunts and New 1918	119
XI.	The Big Show	130
XII.	Last Scene of All	138
XIII.	The Curtain Rings Down	145
	Appendix I	150
	Appendix II	151
	Appendix III	157

ILLUSTRATIONS

"The Gate of Goodbye,"
by F. J. Mortimer, Esq., F.R.P.S. *Frontispiece*

FACING PAGE

Lt.-Col. C. F. Pretor-Pinney, D.S.O. . 19

The Officers in 1915 30

The Warrant Officers and Sergeants in
1915 51

The Corporals in 1915 . . . 62

Lt.-Col. D. E. Prideaux-Brune, D.S.O. 81

Lt.-Col. W. R. Stewart, D.S.O., M.C. 96

H.M. the King and Corporal W. Beesley,
V.C. 131

Sergt. W. Gregg, V.C., D.C.M., M.M.,
and Corporal W. Beesley, V.C. . 131

Lt.-Col. R. A. Mostyn-Owen, D.S.O. 142

FOREWORD

I THINK I am much more in need of an introduction than this book can be. It is only because I had the honour of serving in the 111th Infantry Brigade, to which the 13th R.B. belonged, that I am now honoured with a request to write a Foreword to the tale of the Battalion. Nevertheless I attempt the superfluous task with the greatest possible pleasure.

Let me say at once that to my mind *For the Duration* handsomely fulfils its varied objects. As a smooth unvarnished narrative it is excellent. As an historical record of the formation, the efforts, the achievements, the undying glories of the Battalion, it is admirable. Above all perhaps, it awakens to vivid warmth memories that will never fade but perhaps are growing dim. It does this for me, and I believe it will do so for all other sympathetic readers.

Indeed if I close my eyes upon the page, I am swept backward through time, and all the years between are as nothing. I see again the draughty slopes of Salisbury Plain, the muddy boulevards of Ludgershall, the drooping melancholy fir-trees on top of Windmill Hill. It was here that our Battalion (the 10th Roy. Fus.) first met the 13th R.B.; and we were all of us struck even in those early days by its fine aspect, whether standing rocklike on a full parade, or marching out of camp gay and debonair, with the quick step and alert bearing that are proper to its regimental name. From the beginning it always seemed traditionally correct. We admired the completeness of its assimilation to the splendid parent stock. *Esprit de corps* seemed born with its birth. Every one in its ranks was a Rifleman, and itself was not any Battalion of Infantry, raised and pulled together in an emergency, but visibly, distinctly, unquestionably, a Battalion of the Rifle Brigade.

The assembly of a Division and its mobilization! Those are tremendous affairs. I think we were all impressed, and even found romance and glamour in their unfamiliar details. At a first encounter the pomps and splendours of Divisional Headquarters could not but inspire awe —the red tabs, the red hats—and the portentous notice boards, with "Staff only," "Keep off the Grass," "No admittance on your own business," or similar forbidding captions. Then the snugness, joviality, and happy ease of the R.A.S.C. Again, the mingled profusion and miserliness of that Ordnance Depot at Tidworth. It was like a boot factory in the East End, a severe Harrods, a rather sordid Gamage. One was made to feel exactly like a shop-lifter as soon as one crossed the threshold. Suspicion met one, a blank refusal ushered one out. But if they could not give one what one wanted, they gave one a bit of advice instead—to do without it.

Mr. Rowlands touches lightly on the Windmill Hill episode, and yet it was not without severities. In that strong air and wide space the harsh words of Commanding Officers, Adjutants, and Serjeant-Majors had a more virulent sting in them. It was the last stage of our training, and the educational machine rolled over us with its heaviest pressure. I may be wrong, but I think the strain of those weeks was our most enervating experience. At any rate I am sure that, when told officially we were to cross the Channel in two days, many had a sense of enormous relief. As we plunged into the War, peace sank into our breasts. We were for it at last. What we were leaving behind was far worse than anything we could meet ahead. The Germans might kill us, but they would not nag at us.

Paving-stones and the clatter of limbered waggons, girls singing and laughing, white dusty roads, blazing sunshine, raging thirst, and unopened water-bottles—— From this point onwards to the end of the glorious story I will let the author speak for himself.

But I would like to pay him one more compliment. I admire his abstinence from exaggeration and high colouring. I agree most cordially in his implied condemnation of those books and plays that give a hideously distorted picture of the British Army in the field. This type of literature is a disgrace. The War was terrible enough, Heaven knows, but it was not all mud and blood and blasphemy. Like all great things it had its beauty as well as its nobility, and in the gross insistence on its uglier parts there is an intolerable cruelty to the bereaved relatives of those who in it made the supreme sacrifice. English, German, French have alike been guilty in this respect, as if they purposely sought to tear the hearts and shatter the faith of the parents, wives, sisters who during those fatal years meekly bowed their heads and murmured in tears, "*Dulce et decorum est pro patria mori.*"

Such writers wilfully ignore what was commonly termed "the uplift." But it was there. Uplift! You people of the 13th R.B. all had it. It was not merely being screwed to concert pitch by the sharp goad of danger. You were all living on a higher level than you had ever reached till then. The War had to find men, but in it men found themselves. It drew out of them infinitely more than they had believed was there. Whatever their previous lives, deep inside them there had lain the gleam of light, not noticed, but never extinguished, like the small lamp in a sanctuary chapel, a gleam and no more; or shall I say like the light technically called a leader in old-fashioned illuminations—deep inside one, only a spark, yet ready to glow and flare upward, and fill a man's soul with noble flames.

I wish this book, *For the Duration*, all the success which it undoubtedly deserves.

W. B. MAXWELL

February 1932

LT.-COL. C. F. PRETOR-PINNEY, D.S.O.
First Commanding Officer. Died of Wounds April 28, 1917.

CHAPTER I

SOLDIERS IN THE MAKING

DAY after day in the late summer of 1914, hundreds of men pressed up the High Street of the ancient City of Winchester to the arched West Gate and the Rifle Depot. All sorts and conditions of men—navvies, stockbrokers, artisans, clerks, miners, golf-professionals, artists, students —they besieged the barrack square and waited long hours until the harassed staff could enrol them. At last they were sorted out, and some of them eventually became the 13th (Service) Battalion of the Rifle Brigade, a unit which was destined to gain great distinction on the battlefields of France and Flanders.

So great was the crush of recruits that the facilities at the Depot proved totally inadequate. The dining-rooms which had always been models of military neatness were now cluttered with the remnants of meals served in relays on halfwashed plates. Large batches of men were sent out to sleep—some on the floor of the old Corn Exchange, some in the Red Cross Hospital, pending the arrival of wounded from the Front, some in a hostel patriotically provided by the Countess of Northbrook.

Regular Army Instructors began at once to

make soldiers of us in the crowded barrack square. In little groups we learnt to salute, to mark time, to form fours, to "about-turn" without falling over our feet, and also to double round Winchester before breakfast without losing our wind. We couldn't see the point of these elementary details—we wanted to get on with the War. It was not until our disorderly mob was beginning to develop into a disciplined crowd that the value of all this preliminary training slowly dawned upon us. We had a great many things to learn, and not the least difficult was to know who was, and who was not, entitled to our respectful salutes, so that we "brought the right hand up smartly" whenever we encountered an important personage, from the Colonel to the Sergeant-Major. Another thing which intrigued us was the extremely odd English of some of the N.C.O. Instructors. There was a plump little Corporal we all liked, who, after compiling a nominal roll of men requiring small kit, concluded:

"Fall out them men what ain't had their names took; and them what ain't here to-day fall in again to-morrow!"

It was shameful how we pulled this Corporal's leg. It took him a long time to know his men, so anyone wanting an afternoon off usually took it and had his name answered by a deputy in the rear rank. As a matter of fact we were rather fond of taking French leave, but one evening when some of us had scrambled over the high barrack wall we found, lying in wait for us on the other side, a sentry, who scared us to death by threatening to have us brought before the Commanding Officer. However, a little soothing palm-oil soon settled him, and off we went to the Y.M.C.A. to play billiards.

One great attraction in Winchester was the tuck-shop run by the ladies of the town, where one could have a delightful stodge for threepence. Then there were the historical buildings, and the quaint tombstone outside the Cathedral, warning us to avoid the fate of a soldier of long ago who died through drinking cold small beer. We often lingered in the Cathedral, for its vast Gothic nave, mysterious with slanting sunlight, touched something in our keyed-up minds that we never quite forgot.

* * *

We enjoyed our stay in the ancient capital of England, but we were eager to become pukka soldiers, so it was rather a thrill to leave the L. & S.W. station one dark night early in October for an unknown destination. After a tedious, comfortless journey we were all very glad when the train pulled up in the early morning light at Wendover. Stiff and hungry, we were marched away to Halton Park, a sea of canvas, where we had steaming cocoa served out in basins passed from mouth to mouth; and it was here in the close intimacy of life in bell-tents that we began to know that wonderful fellowship with each other which endured to the end of the War.

We were now a complete Infantry Battalion, established for the duration of the War, and we soon started our training in real earnest. We still had the usual drill, but with instruction in the use of arms, route marches, practice on the miniature range, and skirmishing on the beautiful Chiltern Hills, we felt that we were getting nearer every day to the job for which we had enlisted. How we enjoyed our field exercises on the heights above Wendover, the thrilling charges, the bloodless victories, the midday halt for cocoa and bread and cheese, the range-finding, the lessons in taking cover, and the passing of verbal messages down the line. As a rule these messages were badly distorted in transit, and such a phrase as "Enemy advancing on the right front" would reach the last man as "Enemy dancing in the bright sun."

Here again we heard brutal attacks on our mother tongue. One of the instructors, in explaining the aperture sight of a rifle always asked

"What is a naperture?" and at first he used to supply the answer himself—"Why! A naperture's a nole!" After a while we decided to convince him that we really understood, so whenever he enquired "What is a naperture?" the whole squad would yell delightedly, in chorus—"A naperture's a nole!" Coming to the fixing of bayonets, which in the Rifle Brigade were always called swords, he would tell us dramatically: "When I says 'Fix' yer don't fix; but when I says 'Swords' yer whips 'im out and wops 'im on, and lets 'im bide awhile!" What agonies we went through in our efforts to conceal our amusement, for it was a serious crime to be insolent to a superior officer. Besides, there was always the fear of a more terrible punishment—summary discharge from the Army! In those days a fellow "got his ticket" on the flimsiest pretext, and one man fed up with soldiering, appeared at the medical tent without his false teeth, and mumbled pathetically that he was unable to chew the Army food, so please could he have his discharge? As he was "not likely to become an efficient soldier" he got fired on the spot.

All this time we were being issued with new articles of equipment—dummy rifles, water-bottles, haversacks, and puttees; also boots of a quality that made every march a procession of departed soles. Col. C. F. Pretor-Pinney was in command of the Battalion. Among other officers who joined us at Halton were Col. A. N. Strode Jackson, Col. C. J. Rowlatt, Major P. J. Shears, Captains Bowyer, Chesterton, Rivière, Sampson and Smith, and Lieutenants Bamford, Donaldson, Leggatt, Mackworth, Wiggin and Wood. The Acting R.S.M. was old Fletcher, of the Guards, grey-haired, tall, a veritable martinet. How he loved to demonstrate his vast knowledge of the training manual, and his own importance; how his booming voice rattled our teeth as we stood on parade in holy fear of his authority.

Heavy rains and constant traffic soon converted the camp into a morass; so in November the Battalion moved into huts on a neighbouring site, huts which were later on condemned as unfit for human occupation. Rain used to pour in at night, and in our efforts to keep dry, some of us would move our plank beds away from the walls. Early parades were in force about this time, and when C.S.M. Croutcher appeared at the door of a "B" Company hut one morning, about ten minutes before the "fall in," he was amazed to find one of the fellows still in bed and sound asleep.

"Hi, you! Don't you know you're in the Army now?" asked the Sergeant-Major in his usual dulcet tones.

The Rifleman sat up sleepily, rubbed his eyes, gazed at the surrounding puddle and replied:

"Blow me, Sergeant-Major! I thought I was in the Navy!"

* * *

On November 28, 1914, the Battalion marched to High Wycombe. The first troops to be billeted in the town, we were given a cordial welcome, and in time many hearts were conquered by the charm of the Wycombe lassies. The Saracen's Head became Battalion Headquarters. To balance matters the authorities hired the Baptist Church Schoolroom for lectures, vaccination, inoculation and other inflictions of military life. We now had more officers, among them Major the Marquis of Winchester, Major Sir Foster Cunliffe, Captains Bentinck, Fraser, Lezard, de Laessoe, Morris, Pughe and Vivian, and Lieutenants Boothby, Lawson, Siordet and Waterall. R.S.M. Fletcher left for the 10th Royal Fusiliers, and his place was taken by R.S.M. O'Donnell.

Although the Battalion now reverted to the comforts of civilian life, its soldiering efficiency advanced considerably at High Wycombe; field exercises of various kinds were carried out at Hughenden Park, Daw's Hill and elsewhere;

there were long route marches through charming scenery, instruction in trench digging, night operations on the outskirts of West Wycombe, and ceremonial parades.

There was a touch of home about our billets, especially on wet days, when we would lustily cheer the popular bugle-announcement "No Parades To-day!" Week-end passes were in great demand, but, sad to relate, many of us fell to the temptation to prolong our indulgence of the delights of London, and found ourselves at Orderly Room on our return. The most original excuse for overstaying leave was that of Corpl. Allen of the Transport Section, who, returning a whole week late, was asked by the Commanding Officer if he had anything to say.

"Yes, sir," replied the Corporal meekly, "I lost the train!"

Another story, but one with a different moral, concerns the men of "B" Company, who marched to Taplow and visited the home of Viscountess Astor. After allowing the men to eat their haversack rations in the glorious park surrounding Cliveden Grange, Lady Astor suggested that they might like some refreshment, and as her views on Strong Drink were not so well known in those days, it was an expectant crowd which lined up at the side of the great house. Then a door opened quietly. Each man in turn stepped forward and was presented with two Woodbines —and a glass of lemonade. With commendable tact the Company Commander marched his men away very soon afterwards.

After a stay of more than four months at High Wycombe, we received orders to proceed to Salisbury Plain. So ended one of the happiest episodes in the history of the old Battalion, and on the morning of April 9, 1915, amid tender farewells from the large crowd which had gathered at the station, we set out on the last stage of our training in England.

*   *   *

On rising ground known as Windmill Hill, near the village of Ludgershall, we found a new home. The change from billet to bell-tent was none too welcome. Many a tent succumbed to the lashing of April winds, and the sorrows of the night were often followed in the morning by the joy of sorting out legs, equipment, shaving soap and mother's cake.

Up till then most of us had been garbed in convict-like uniforms of navy blue, owing to the shortage of khaki. Now came the issue of field-service dress of the proper colour, real rifles, entrenching tools and all the paraphernalia of war. Stuffed sacks suspended from gallows reminded us of the grim realism of bayonet-fighting. Across the dusty road which skirted the camp was a rifle-range, where budding marksmen tried out their skill, and at one end of the tent lines was a collection of mules who responded lustily to all the bugle-calls. Again the dear old Army menu. Again the anxious enquiry of the Orderly Officer—"any complaints?" At night from the lighted tents songs echoed down the lines—"When Irish Eyes are Smiling," "Sweet and Low," "The Sunshine of your Smile," "Little Grey Home in the West," and all the other old favourites. After the last lingering notes of the final bugle-call would come a banging on the canvas, an imperious command, "Lights Out There!" and then a great silence.

Discipline became stricter as the days went by. There was keen competition for the best turn-out for the daily camp-guards, and the Adjutant's choice sometimes rested on a show of teeth and finger-nails. Route marches across the Plain were often on the programme; there were many visits to the rifle butts beyond Tidworth, and field operations, too, including a week's manœuvres, which started with a march to Hungerford one Monday morning. There the rain kept us indoors during the whole of the following day, but that night, about twelve o'clock, the streets of the old Wiltshire town echoed to the sound of marching feet. On through the darkness we moved in shadowy ranks, halting now and then on the outskirts of some village that had long since gone to sleep, and on again through the night, till, as we emerged from Savernake Forest, the finger of dawn was deftly touching the tall trees and the birds were beginning their songs. In a little while we came to the village of Pewsey, where we found welcome signs of breakfast and a resting-place for weary heads.

The week's operations ended on the Friday afternoon, a day of blazing heat, with clouds of dust rising from the long hedgeless road that stretched from Collingbourne Ducis, and to the tune of "Over the Hills and Far Away" Sergeant Billy Dean and his merry buglers led the Battalion back to the gentle slopes of Windmill Hill.

In June it was rumoured that we were going to Gallipoli. That old campaigner, Jerry Bond, Company Storeman and a champion romancer, had vowed that he had seen "piles and piles of tropical helmets in the Quartermaster's Stores"; hence the story that we were bound for the East. Just then all kinds of tales were in circulation—most of them the result of whispered conversation in a certain part of the camp where the smell of chloride of lime seemed to induce men to "talk of many things." These yarns all helped to enliven our leisure moments, so did the games of "House" controlled by a fellow with a big voice, who kept on shouting that a winning number was "*clickety-click*" and that "top of the 'ouse" was ninety.

We also found entertainment at the occasional concerts arranged by the Padre, the Rev. H. E. Wynn, at one of which we saw Capt. Chesterton give a masterly impersonation of a brother officer coming on parade, monocled and loaded up like a Christmas-tree. Week-end passes, too, sustained the spirit of the troops, and it was really remarkable how many Riflemen succeeded in travelling to Waterloo for a few pence, merely by the practice of a little ingenuity when the ticket collector came along.

In the last week of July 1915 we heard the news, official this time, that we should shortly be leaving for the Front, and we all felt thrilled at the prospect of going overseas. One can still see the late Col. Pretor-Pinney addressing the Battalion, his voice a little shaken with emotion. A fine soldier, justly proud of his officers and men, he realized that in the near future changes must inevitably occur in the personnel of that wonderful unit of Kitchener's Army.

At four o'clock on the morning of July 29th, réveillé was sounded, for the last time on Salisbury Plain, in the camp of the 13th Rifle Brigade.

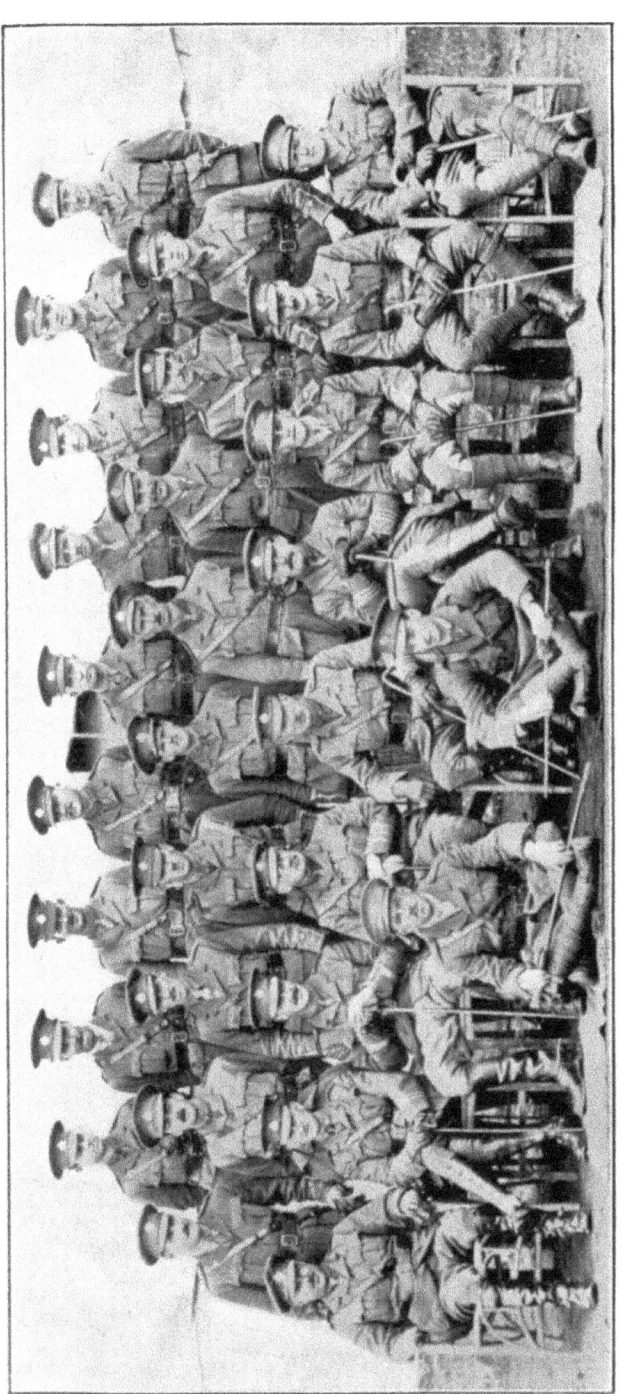

THE OFFICERS. *Salisbury Plain,* 1915.

By 10 a.m. the Battalion and its baggage had left for Southampton Docks.

When we embarked that evening the sun had laid a path of beaten gold along the sea. Snatches of song drifted back to the shore as *Mona's Queen* slid quietly down the Solent, carrying southwards many who would not look again on the land of their birth.

CHAPTER II

EARLY DAYS IN FRANCE

ON July 30, 1915, at six o'clock in the morning, *Mona's Queen* drew alongside the quay at Havre and delivered us up to the B.E.F. Only the sun offered greetings. There were no pretty girls, no flowers, no cheering. Just a workaday crowd who appeared to have lost all interest in the coming and going of soldiers. Early though it was, the day was already hot, and with everyone carrying an overweighted pack, after the style of old Atlas, we sweated along to a camp that seemed miles away from the docks. Next morning came a march to the station, where all "other ranks" were introduced to a form of travel advertised thus on the door of each wagon:

| CHEVAUX (en long) | 8 |
| HOMMES | 35–40 |

We all clambered in at 10.45 a.m., and for hours had to listen to small boys who were calling out "*Chocolats! Biscuits!*" and "*My seester ... she promenade avec vous ce soir.*"

The train eventually crawled out at 2 p.m. The weather was perfect, and everybody was happy enough at first. Our legs—at least the legs of the men who had gained the vantage positions—dangled through the open doorway, and the speed of the train gave us a chance to study the wild flowers which grew in profusion along the permanent way. Every now and then the train would stop, but there was no knowing for how long, as the movements of the State Railway in those days were not directed by the desires or designs of the British Army. Towards evening we pulled up at Hazebrouck, and as there was every promise that the stop would be a long one, a large crowd of us tumbled out on to the platform to fill our empty water-bottles, many leaving their boots behind in the train. Suddenly, without warning, the engine started to move. Amid agonized cries from the departing and louder screams from the abandoned, it slowly gathered speed, and for the moment it looked as if the Battalion was going to be decimated before reaching the Front. Great was the agitation until the lost sheep were at last restored to the fold.

Each wagon had a complement of forty men, and after being jammed together for several hours, with nothing but bare boards or our packs to sit on, we were glad when another stop was made and café cognac was served out by a party of French soldiers.

The train toiled on into the night, the ancient rolling-stock grinding out a song that seemed to say, "Bump-a-bit—stop-a-bit—*P—B—I—*!" After eighteen hours of this, with aching bones, and rations nearly exhausted, we arrived at last at the little station of Watten. Then came a march to a spot where peace reigned supreme. Aged folk were bending their backs in the fields, and poplars stood sentinel in the morning light, while here and there a little estaminet advertised the virtues of *Dubonnet* and *Byrrh*. Weary-eyed as we were, we realized that we were in France at last.

Two Companies went into billets in the village of Mentque, the other two Companies, with Headquarters, going on to Nortbecourt. Gradually we gained new impressions of France. All the women seemed plain, fat and corsetless; all the little farms huddled lovingly about their pungent middens; all the barns, built of mud and straw, were alive with fleas.

On the morning of August 4th, a year after England declared war, we started our long trek to the Front. Marching via St. Omer and Arques, we reached the village of Campagne the same afternoon. There was a canal on the outskirts of this village, and many of the lads were eager to enjoy a dip; but a soldier's pack did not carry bathing-kit and there were ladies in the vicinity. However, it was soon apparent that the onlookers in no way shared our embarrassment, so in we all went. Indeed, this Gallic indifference to the conventions often shocked our English minds, though as time went on we got case-hardened.

Next morning the Battalion moved forward. It was a sweltering day, and ahead was a long straight road of poplars. Hour after hour passed under a scorching sun, the same horizon in view, the same crippling cobbles underfoot. Each kilometre seemed to grow in length, sweat was pouring down our faces in long trickles, packs grew heavier, rifle slings kept on slipping, butts bumped into knees, and still no sign of our journey's end. All very well for the Sergeant to say "left right, left right"; all very well for the Adjutant to glare at the men who broke step and cursed him under their breath. A number of men, beaten by the heat and the *pavé* fell by the wayside, much to the annoyance of some Brass Hats who were looking down on the scene from comfortable saddles. Then, in the late afternoon, we met the billeting party, who had gone on in advance to prepare a home for the Battalion in the village of St. Sylvestre Cappel. The next ten days passed pleasantly enough in that charming district, despite many small hardships like the bread ration, then a loaf for every ten men, chlorinated water, and our first troubles with the primitive gas-mask of that period. We also had to endure daily parades for the purpose of hearing the miserable fate of men found guilty of cowardice, desertion, and other offences punishable with death—apparently it had been decreed that all these lamentable details should be recited in full so as to provide necessary stimulus to the morale of the men just out from England!

While the Battalion was at St. Sylvestre, a digging party was sent to the Front to work in the Canadian Divisional area. This party, in charge of Major the Marquis of Winchester, came under fire, and a few men were wounded by shrapnel. On August 16th the Battalion marched to Bailleul, where the night was spent in billets of various kinds, including a theatre, and next day a move was made to Le Bizet, on the outskirts of Armentières.

Now came the real thing. The boom of artillery grew more distinct and the rat-tat-tat of machine-guns sounded very near; battered windows had been patched with rags, and over the way was the skeleton of a farmhouse which shielded the breech of an 18-pounder.

Early on the morning of August 18th, "A" and "B" Companies went into the front line, and started to receive instruction in trench duties from the 6th Queens and 6th Buffs. "C" and "D" Companies were acting as digging parties just behind. Next morning the front-line Companies came out of the trenches and the other two Companies took their place. The same night Rfn. C. H. Wall, of "D" Company, was killed —the first serious casualty in the Battalion. This daily change-over of duties proceeded for some time, and for the fellows in the line there was comparative peace in the daytime, so long as heads remained below the parapet, but once darkness set in, listening patrols would crawl out on their bellies into No Man's Land and all sorts of missiles whistled overhead, provoking a wholesale display of wind-up. Sometimes there would be a miniature earthquake, as on the occasion when Harry Rockall, an "old sweat," known to everybody in the Battalion, experienced premature burial, so that for a time it was all earth and no Rockall; but shovels were quickly requisitioned, and to the accompaniment of language suited to both the occasion and the man, he was dug out. Once again was it proved that "old soldiers never die," and Rockall was spared to fight another day and eventually to become the soldiers' friend in the Quartermaster's Stores.

We moved away from this part of the line on August 25th, and after staying two nights at Bailleul, we boarded the train at Godewaersvelde to be jolted on to Doullens, which we reached late the same evening, August 27th. The march from the station led up a long steep hill, productive of much sweat and swearing, but at last, just on midnight, we arrived at Halloy, where we had waterproof sheets for palliasses and the starry sky for roof. Here we stayed for four days and then marched to St. Amand, passing through the trim little town of Pas. We were now in the Gommecourt sector.

CHAPTER III

GOMMECOURT 1915

DURING the afternoon of September 2nd, officers and Platoon sergeants visited the trenches held by the French in front of Hannescamps. At nine-thirty the same night we started out for the line, and, marching via Pommier and Bienvillers, we passed through a wide trench which ran alongside the main road leading to Hannescamps. We were now less than a mile from the German trenches. The village lay in a pool of moonlight as we moved quietly between the deserted houses; and above the broken wall of the little church, a crucifix hung in dark outline against a pale-green sky. The cross had survived the storm of war, and to many an English soldier that night it was a sign and portent.

We now entered the communication trench, a lane so narrow that our packs brushed the crumbling soil on either side, as we made our way into the front line. The French troops soon handed over, leaving British Tommies in possession of this sector for the first time in the history of the War; but when morning came it was apparent at once that much remained to be done to strengthen the position and improve the sanitation. The following night "B" Company moved out and took over the trenches in front of Fonquevillers, a village on the right, which in happier times must have been a place of great charm. The communication trench from the village to the front line began in an orchard, so that whenever any of the boys had to go back to collect R.E. material during those autumn days, they usually returned to the line with pockets full of apples.

One of the first casualties in this sector was Corpl. J. B. Dent, of "C" Company, who was shot through the head by a sniper and died the next day. He was a tall, cultured fellow who preferred serving in the ranks to taking up a commission, and his death was a great shock to us, who were not yet inured to the cruelty of war. In those early days steel helmets were among the many things we had to do without. Rifle ammunition, too, was doled out in small quantities and we had to collect the empty cases in sandbags to be sent back for refilling, while the batteries behind, when asked to reply to the enemy's bombardment of our trenches would often report apologetically, "Sorry, but we've already used up our day's allowance of shells!"

The 13th K.R.R.C. came into the line after we had been there for eight days, and we then went back to Bienvillers. During the next four days we sent working parties up to Hannescamps and we then learned the solemn truth that everyone in a Field Company of Royal Engineers was a Director when the business in hand was trench-digging.

On handing over our billets in Bienvillers to the 6th Bedfords, we became reserve troops and marched to Humbercamps. Here we experienced a welcome change from Forward Area conditions —old people were working in the fields unperturbed by the nearness of war, while a few small shops and estaminets still carried on. Another unexpected amenity was the Divisional Canteen at Gaudiempré. There were also the baths at Pas, where in a brewery were great vats now filled with soapy water and naked Tommies. It was great fun chasing the soap in those huge vats; but our enjoyment was tinged with regret that a building once dedicated to hops should now be used in dealing with hoppers.

The Battle of Loos opened on September 25th, and as the Battalion had been warned to hold itself in readiness to move off at short notice everybody was standing by, in fighting order. The Church Parade that Sunday morning seemed to have especial significance; letters were written to the folk at home, and there was a feeling of hushed expectancy as day passed into evening and lights went out in the scattered billets. However, the anticipated move northwards did not take place, and a few days later we marched back to the trenches which we had left three weeks before. A great calamity now occurred. Some reinforcements from England had just arrived, and on their very first night in the line all those posted to "B" Company were detailed to go and collect rations in the village of Fonquevillers. Since the communication trench was then in a frightful mess following heavy rains, they had to make their way over the top, and in the inky darkness the fellow in charge of the rum jar arrived back in the front line sooner than he expected, so suddenly in fact that he landed head first in a sump-hole. Alas! the shock caused him to lose his hold on the S.R.D., and when he had regained his feet the precious jar was reported missing. The flood of liquid mud he met during his ducking was not to be compared with the torrent of strong language released that night by his dispirited comrades. It was subsequently whispered that the Sergeant-Major spent long hours fishing in that sump-hole, but whether or not he landed a catch, none but he and a few intimates ever knew. The men were gravely suspicious about it.

On the night of October 1st a patrol went out and encountered a strong party of Germans in No Man's Land. A sharp fight ensued and when Lieut. A. F. H. Wiggin, who was wounded, brought the patrol back it was found that Corpl. F. Wicking and Rfn. W. Roberts, both of "C" Company, were missing.

At the end of this tour of the line, the Battalion went back to Bienvillers, and subsequently marched to billets in the village of Berles-au-Bois. It was here that an amusing experience befell Rfn. M. Cornforth, who, wanting to know his way to Battalion Headquarters, accosted a French sentry.

"Voulez-vous me dire s'il vous plaît," he asked in his best school French, *"le . . . le chemin . . . vers le Mairie?"*

The *poilu* grinned at him broadly.

"Yus, mate," he replied, in excellent Cockney. "Yer tike the first turning on the left, past the little boozer on the roight, and there yer are!"

Cornforth then discovered that the sentry, although a private in the French Army, was in fact an Englishman.

After a period of "digging under the R.E."—to quote Battalion orders—we proceeded to St. Amand, where we indulged in more digging, this time on the Corps line. Then came another tour of the trenches at Hannescamps and Fonquevillers. On the night of October 23rd one of our patrols ran into a strong party of Germans, armed with bombs, and after a stiff fight withdrew. Our casualties were one man wounded and two missing—Corpl. Porter and Rfn. Ollerhead.

The jolly old War continued on monotonous lines during the next four or five weeks, trips to the trenches alternating for us with spells in billets at Bienvillers and Humbercamps. November 3rd was a red-letter day, as leave to England began. Leave! Blessed word! How it recalled the lights of London and the windswept hills at home!

With the object of keeping alive the fighting spirit of the troops, there were further adventures into No Man's Land, and on the night of November 20th an operation on a grand scale was carried out. There were two large patrolling parties, one under 2nd Lieut. D. F. Bruce, the other in charge of 2nd Lieut. J. Morris. As the first party proceeded along the Hannescamps ravine to lie in wait for any hostile patrol that might be venturing out, the second crept along the Essarts road, the intention being to wedge the enemy between them if possible. Presently our leading patrol noticed a party of about seventy Germans, and after getting into a fighting position they gave the enemy a burst of rapid fire. There were cries and shouted orders from the Germans, followed by a shower of bombs and volleys of rifle-fire. Mr. Bruce had sent back for reinforcements and when these came up with 2nd Lieut. C. J. Rowlatt, the "charge" was given and the retiring enemy was scattered in all directions. At the same moment our Artillery opened fire with good effect. This successful operation was officially commended, but unfortunately two members of Mr. Rowlatt's party were wounded, one fatally.

During the weeks that followed, rain fell incessantly and the front line was scarcely habitable. Some of the communication trenches had collapsed completely, while others were knee-deep in liquid mud, so that at night traffic to and from the front line usually took to the open. Discomfort in the firebays was acute, yet in spite of everything the men maintained a spirit of good humour. It was during this period that we were informed one dark night that an Indian Prince was on his way round the trenches, and we were much impressed to see a tall figure in a turban, accompanied by aides-de-camps and the Company Commander, inspecting the various firebays and saps and questioning officers and men in broken English. The occasion was obviously one of great importance. It was not till the next day that the truth came out. The whole thing had been a legpull, and the "Eastern Potentate" one of our own officers from Battalion Headquarters.

The men, too, had their little joke, often at

the expense of the N.C.O.'s. There was poor Sergt. Faulkner, who had suggested that a certain bay could be much improved by a wooden firestep.

"Yes, Sergeant," agreed one of the boys. "I can't help wondering why the N.C.O.'s haven't put their heads together!"

At that time the Battalion used to come out of the trenches just before dawn, and as we reached the village of Bienvillers the early morning light would be filtering through the open doorways of the barns that were to be our billets during the next six days. On one of these winter mornings, soon after our breakfast of bread and cheese, or bacon, the Orderly Sergeant came round to announce a Commanding Officer's inspection at two o'clock. Stained with mud from head to foot, worn out and fed up, none of us took kindly to the idea of presenting an immaculate appearance on parade in a few hours' time, and it was natural perhaps that in our clean-up many of us scamped the business of shaving. At the appointed hour the troops were lined up in the muddy road. When Col. Pretor-Pinney appeared to inspect No 8 Platoon, he noticed one exceptionally dark chin, and, turning to the Sergeant-Major, said severely,

"Here's a man who hasn't had a shave. Take his name and number!"

"Name and number?" demanded the Sergeant-Major.

The unlucky one meekly said:

"S.4054. Morgan E."

The C.O. then passed along the front file, happened to look back, and stretched out a reproachful finger.

"There's another man, Sergeant-Major, who hasn't had a shave. Take his name and number!"

"Name and number?" demanded the Sergeant-Major.

Once again came the quiet confession,

"S.4054. Morgan E."

Walking now between the two files, Col. Pretor-Pinney had a rear view of the men in front. The hairy face of poor Rfn. Morgan assumed a look of deep melancholy as once more the C.O. pointed to him and in pained tones remarked,

"Why, Sergeant-Major, there's yet another man who hasn't had a shave. Take his name and number!"

By this time the men in the rear rank were approaching a state of apoplexy, due to their efforts to control their laughter.

Morgan used to relate this story in his own inimitable way, but he will tell it no more, alas, for he was severely wounded a week before the Armistice and died four years later.

*   *   *

How often one lives again that unforgettable experience, a winter night in the trenches . . .

It is dusk. On the order "Stand-to!" you grab your rifle, mount the firestep, and gaze out across the grey landscape that is No Man's Land, with the dark mass of Adinfer Wood in the distance and the ruins of Monchy beyond. In the fading light, in the near foreground, you see the twisted shapes of barbed wire and the wooden cross and képi that mark the grave of a soldier of France who died here long months ago. Some fool lets off his rifle, and German machine-guns start traversing. The bullets skim the sandbags, and while you press yourself against the trench wall, waiting for the racket to end, Lewis guns from behind decide to reply. Our fellows are in humorous mood to-night as their answer is a merry pom-tiddley-om-pom; pom-tiddley-om-pom; pom-pom! *Away on the right, gun flashes are lighting the sky. It has started to rain. Our artillery are now shelling the "Z," and a message is passed down that a patrol is going out at eight o'clock and that the password is "Kismet."*

The order "Stand down" is heard and you then line up for your rum. It's given you in a mug—a little drop at the bottom—you gulp it down, and if you're lucky enough not to be next for sentry duty or included in the nightly ration party, you slip back into your dug-out, a shelter so flimsy that one direct hit, and you'd be "put out of mess."

As you push back the ragged bit of brown blanket that serves for your door, you dimly see two fellows lying asleep on short wire beds, their feet dangling over a pool of water beneath. The charcoal brazier is out, and in the light of a guttering candle you start writing a letter, only to find that the damp in your tunic pocket has stuck down your only green envelope, so you decide to send a Field Post-Card instead. You throw yourself down on the remaining wire bed, which is sagging badly in the middle, prop your head on a haversack and pull your greatcoat over you, and soon you realize the presence of crowds of little parasites now coming out of hiding in the seams of your clothes. You try to sleep but cannot. So you watch the rats on the rough shelf above, big fellows who seem to be scheming how to get that sandbag of rations prudently suspended in mid-air. . . .

It is two ack emma. Your turn at sentry duty has come round. How tired you are after a day spent in cleaning and repairing the firebay and your bit of the communication trench—your limbs are one dead ache, and your fingers are icy cold. The fellow you relieve says "Hullo, mate! Glad you've come!" and mumbles something about movement out there, near the barbed wire. "You're getting balmy, lad!" you tell him; but after he's gone you begin to see things yourself. Yes, there it is—a crouching form moving ever so slightly, but moving all right. When the Sergeant comes round, you report what you've seen, but he only advises you not to be silly, adding that all those barbed wire pickets are firmly fixed in the ground. The rain shoots off the waterproof sheet you have made into a cape and soaks through your puttees. You stamp your feet to try and get them warm. You blow on your mittened hands and pull tight your "woolly bear"—one of the fur jackets just issued to the front line troops. You'd give anything for a smoke, but dare not chance it in case you're caught. . . .

You return to the dug-out at last, your legs stiff with the wet and the cold, you light the Tommy cooker you've just had from home, and settle down to a meal of hard biscuits, cheese and tea. You decide on "kip" but sleep is a long time coming. After dozing awhile you hear the "Stand-to" again, and you then realize wearily that another day has begun. . . .

* * *

On December 17th, now back in Bienvillers, we heard the news that one of the working parties, which we sent out daily to the front line, had met with disaster. It was a party consisting of men from various companies, and having finished their task they were assembling near Piccadilly Circus, in Hannescamps, when a salvo of shells crashed in their midst. The N.C.O. in charge, Sergt. Bennett, tried at once to collect his scattered men, but alas, he found that five

THE WARRANT OFFICERS AND SERGEANTS. *Salisbury Plain,* 1915.

were already dead and two beyond all hope. The poor fellows killed were Rfn. Griffiths of "A" Company, Rfn. Lewis of "D" Company, and Riflemen Cox, Mayhook and Watts of "B" Company. Rfn. Bentley and Bugler Auger, both of "B," died of wounds the next day. This was the biggest blow the Battalion had yet received and we all felt it keenly.

When Christmas Day arrived we were in Humbercamps, and out of the line. After "Divine Service," the only celebration mentioned in the Battalion's official record of December 25th, we indulged in all the boisterous fun which we had associated with Christmas since the days of our childhood, particularly those of us who were still in our teens. The cooks did their best that day, providing a welcome "roast" instead of the recurrent "gippo"; pudding, too, made from ration biscuits—crushed, so one wag said, by the wheels of an Army limber. The village reserves of beer, *vin rouge* and *vin blanc* were brought up in great force, and the decrepit beams of every barn echoed with singing and laughter as the hours passed. One platoon decided that Christmas could not be properly celebrated without a fire, so the mouldy-looking door of a cartshed was commandeered and set alight in an old rusty bucket. Next day the irate farmer handed in his bill for the damage. It was 250 francs, but, like most of his compatriots, he seemed quite happy to accept a much smaller sum, on this occasion 75 francs.

We returned to the trenches soon afterwards. During the following weeks, nothing of much importance happened until January 28th, when the 48th Division, who were holding the line on the right of Fonquevillers, reported that they were being severely "strafed." Suddenly the gas alarm was given, the improvised gongs were sounded, and each man quickly donned his P.H. helmet, a sticky bag of grey flannel that enclosed the head and tucked into the neck of one's tunic. After remaining on the firestep for nearly an hour, in a state of wind-up and semi-suffocation, we were ordered to Stand-down and take off our masks, and when we did, everybody was suspicious about that alarm. There was certainly a sickly smell in one of the firebays, yet it was rather significant that one of the men in that platoon, Rfn. Phipps, had not put in an appearance at all during the Stand-to; there he was in his dug-out, calmly frying a red herring which he had received with the mail the previous night, and there, too, was the fount and origin of the unlovely odour which had so put the breeze up the troops!

Rfn. Phipps, better known as "Chelsea," was a homely-looking old chap, who had put back his age fifteen years when he joined up in 1914, and in confidential mood he would confess to having a son in the trenches.

On January 31st, in the late afternoon, the enemy started shelling "C" Company's trenches, and destroyed an Artillery O.P., killing its occupants, a gunner officer and Capt. A. G. Lezard. This was our last day in the Gommecourt sector. Capt. Lezard had come all the way from South Africa to do his bit in the War—a charming officer, bluff and hearty, and adored by his men. It was night when we buried him in the communal cemetery of Bienvillers. With slow, muffled, tread we carried him up the village street, whilst someone swung a lantern in front and guns boomed and flared on our left. We were reminded of the burial of that other rifleman, Sir John Moore, on a January night like this—

> By the struggling moonbeam's misty light,
> And the lantern dimly burning.
>
> No useless coffin enclosed his breast,
> Not in sheet nor in shroud we wound him;
> But he lay like a warrior taking his rest,
> With his martial cloak around him.

CHAPTER IV

LE GASTINEAU—AUXI—AND BACK AGAIN

A PERIOD in billets was suddenly cut short by an order to move to another part of the line, and late on the night of February 12, 1916, we took over the trenches at Le Gastineau, a bleak spot some six or seven miles north of the Gommecourt sector. The War in this new area had apparently been conducted on the basis of "live and let live," as there was little sign of activity on either side. Indeed, we were told by the French troops before they left that a well in No Man's Land could be used without hindrance, as arrangements had been made with the Germans; but, in accordance with a good old British custom, we soon gingered things up and thereafter no water was drawn from that well.

This was an extraordinary bit of line, one part of it running down a ravine and up the other side; and with the enemy snipers perched on higher ground and always on the look-out for a human target, life in some of our firebays hung by a very thin thread. To make matters worse, the liquid mud would stream down those sloping trenches in rivers, whilst the poor devils down below had hard work to cope with it. Even the cooks found life none too pleasant, and "B" Company's travelling kitchen lived up to its descriptive name one day, so hot was the pace set by old Jerry's artillery.

At first, our rest barns were in Bailleulmont, just two miles down a road where, on dark winter nights, the transport men raced their limbers round bumpy corners which tested both driving skill and vocabulary. Somehow the rough life of the trenches did not fit in with the routine out of the line, and many men were "crimed" for offences that seemed very trivial to fighting troops. Among the early arrivals at Orderly Room, in the old Marie of Bailleulmont, was a young Rifleman (now the well-known actor, Aubrey Dexter) who, trying to obtain medical treatment at the aid-post, was rewarded with "medicine and duty," plus a charge of "reporting sick without cause"; but before the Battalion was back in the trenches, he found himself before the C.O. once more, this time on two charges, (1) "absenting himself from billet," and (2) "failing to report sick!" In giving him a sentence of seven days Field Punishment Number Two, military justice was apparently done, but it rather baffled the mind of a youth still only seventeen.

Snow arrived early in March. It was a pretty sight to see the barbed wire all festooned with fairy whiteness; but everyone agreed that snow looked better on Christmas-cards. Wintry conditions remained for some time, and although feet were anointed twice a day with anti-frostbite grease, the foundations of the Battalion were sorely tested; in fact, sore feet and creaking limbs gave us such an aged appearance that the little groups of Riflemen who wearily made their way back from the trenches at the end of six days could not have been recognized as the same smart lads who had looked so spick and span in their billets a short while before. White suits were ordered for night patrols, but by the time that the wheels of the Ordnance Department had made one complete revolution, those suits were no longer wanted, as a thaw had set in and the landscape was again a dull grey.

The volume of mud now grew to an alarming extent, and the trenches were in such a swampy mess that when Platoon Commanders made their nightly tours of the firebays, they usually travelled along the parapet, with the result that a sentry would often get jumpy when he saw an indistinguishable figure coming from the direction of the enemy. One very dark night 2nd Lieut. E. B. Boothby fell off the sandbags into a sumphole, and on clambering out, half-blinded with mud, found a gleaming bayonet within an inch of his tummy. It is difficult to say which was the more scared, officer or sentry. At any rate, recognition led to an outburst of mutual swearing, but happily a condition of "good order and military discipline" was soon restored on "C" Company's front. Boothby was an officer long remembered for his monocle, his breezy language and his sheer inability to "crime" the worst offender. What a blow his death was on the Somme to all the survivors in his Platoon, including the devoted batman with whom he had violent quarrels, followed each time by complete reconciliation and stronger friendship.

It was during this tour of the line that "B" Company lost Rfn. R. Pengelly, a gallant fellow, killed by a sniper's bullet as he went to the aid of a wounded comrade. A successful journalist, and a married man with children, he had already reached an age that might have kept him guarding bridges at home, when he decided that his proper place was in the trenches. Late at night we buried him in the garden of a ruined farmhouse used as Battalion Headquarters, with a chilly wind blowing across the open grave, and stray shots pinging over from the German line. The sky would brighten at fitful intervals as a Verey light hovered over No Man's Land like some evil bird seeking after its prey. We stood there, a little company of mourners, thinking of poor Pengelly and his people at home, and conscious of the haunting words of the burial service and of the figure of the padre in his surplice, as the lights flickered and died, leaving us in darkness.

Conditions in the front line remained bad, and one poor chap, overcome by the exposure and the hard toil of the trenches, was found dead in his dug-out early one morning. The officers did all they could to give us some spark of comfort, among them the late Capt. Bentinck, who used to wander back to the village in the rear and return loaded up with little treats for his men. He and his beloved signallers shared a wonderful comradeship, and many were the re-assuring notes which he addressed to parents and wives and slipped in with the letters given him to censor.

One morning in March, Battalion Headquarters and the Support Line were subjected to a heavy bombardment, but considering that over ninety H.E. shells were fired by the enemy in just over an hour, the damage done was surprisingly small. Headquarters escaped altogether, but one of the dug-outs in the Support Line received a direct hit, and Riflemen Raines, Pitt and Smith were killed, whilst three other members of "C" Company in that dug-out were severely wounded.

* * *

We were now back in our barns in Bailleulmont, but not for long, as on March 18th we set out for a place which proved a veritable haven of peace. The route was via La Herlière, Warlincourt, Halloy, Occoches, Mezerolles and Wavans, and after staying at most of these villages, sometimes for a night, sometimes longer, we eventually reached Auxi-le-Château, an attractive little town where the Third Army School of Training had been established. We were now attached to this school, and the "spit and polish" régime soon began, since the honour of the 13th Rifle Brigade, chosen out of the whole Division as a Demonstration Battalion, was at stake. So badges and buckles were brightened, boots shone with Cherry Blossom, entrenching tool handles revealed their pristine whiteness after much scrubbing, and straps and rifles glistened in the spring sunshine. For the education of the officers in training at the school, we demonstrated the Attack, and showed them how Company Drill should be done. We were also made to practise saluting, carefully, meticulously, over and over again, until the lads groaned under the wearisome repetition. It was the butt of many jokes. Said one fellow, imitating the speech of one of our N.C.O. Instructors of 1914, "About this serluting: What I says is, yer don't take it serious enough. Look at me, for example—I always chucks one up every time I meets an object of respect. Don't matter if it's a pretty girl, a Solomon in all his glory—meaning a ruddy General—or a glass of beer!"

The demonstrations of the attack were more serious affairs. There were first waves and second waves, there were bombers and Lewis gunners, and moppers-up, and so on and so on. But even these serious shows had an amusing turn sometimes, as happened one day when our display was attended by subalterns and their instructors, and a collection of high personages all in red and gold and medal ribbons. The first wave had just halted, and the whole of the party was lying prone when an officer of high rank came along. He addressed a recumbent figure,

"Are you a bomber?"
"No, sir."
"Are you a Lewis gunner?"
"No, sir."
"Are you a mopper-up?"
"No, sir."
"Then what the devil are you, man?"
"I'm the Sergeant-Major, sir!"

*   *   *

Life was very pleasant during that springtime. It was joy to see a pretty face, to buy

LE GASTINEAU—AUXI—AND BACK AGAIN

pâtisserie in one of the shops, to have gorges of *des œufs et pommes de terre frites*, to make trips to Abbeville, to wander in the country where young corn was growing in the fields, to hear larks singing in the sunshine and the Angelus at evening instead of the growl of the guns. In the spring of each later year of the War many of us would sigh,

"Oh, to be in Auxi, now that April's there!"

Alas! All happy days in a warrior's life are sorrowfully brief, and though our step seemed light, our hearts were bowed down as we swung past the little Hôtel de Ville on the morning of April 29th and marched our way back to the trenches.

*   *   *

After spending a couple of days in support billets at Berles-au-Bois, and a few more in Bailleulval, we returned to the Gastineau sector. On coming out of the line we went back to Bailleulval, and for some months subsequently we made that village our rest position. During our first period in billets we supplied large working parties, who were engaged in digging a new trench in front of the existing front line, and this new bit of architecture soon attracted the attention of the German Artillery, so that one night a digging party of the 13th K.R.R.C. was heavily shelled.

The merry month of May came to an end, and no important incident occurred until the night of June 4th, when a patrol in charge of 2nd Lieut. W. W. Nothard ran into a small crowd of Germans in the Berles ravine, and after a short, sharp fight routed them. Two German dead were left behind, both young soldiers of the 76th Infantry Regiment, one a flaxen-haired youth named Heinrich Petersen, who had been a University student, and in whose pocket was a letter from his mother imploring him to take care of himself. Poor woman! we all felt sorry that she would never again see her boy.

Life was now beginning to assume a more pleasing aspect. The rainy season had ended, so that the soil was hardening, and at "Stand-to" in the morning one could hear the birds tuning up and see here and there a poppy among the barbed wire. In the village behind, the peasants in their cottage gardens, bright with sweet-williams and stocks and old-fashioned roses, were looking much more cheerful.

Prior to our next tour of the line we sent large parties each night to the trenches to carry gas cylinders. Each of these cylinders, weighing 160 pounds, was carried by two men, who, being also encumbered with their rifles and bandoliers, would let forth great floods of sweat and language as they hauled their loads into position

THE CORPORALS, *Salisbury Plain*, 1915.

under the supervision of the R.E.'s, making a clangour that must have been heard by the Germans.

One night late in June, now back in the line, we sent out a large patrol with the object of raiding a listening post, but when cutting the enemy's wire they were challenged, and in the fight which followed 2nd Lieut. Nothard was severely wounded by a bomb. It was sheer bad luck for our fellows to find the German sentries on the alert, but they managed nevertheless to inflict many casualties on the enemy.

From now till the end of the month the normal routine of the trenches was varied by much racket on both sides. With the wind blowing from the West, a warning would come down our line that gas was about to be discharged from the cylinders which we had so laboriously helped to instal, and whilst everybody stood-to in gas-masks, small parties would crawl out over the parapet as a grey-green cloud was settling down on the enemy trenches. Did our patrols find, on the other side, whole firebays filled with dead Germans, all wearing a ghastly complexion? Oh, no! What they did find was a crowd of very active Jerries, each wearing his gas-protector (and, no doubt, a derisive grin beneath it).

We now got news that a Military Cross had been awarded to 2nd Lieut. D. F. Bruce, the first member of the Battalion to receive official recognition of gallantry in the field. This young officer, who was at Marlborough at the outbreak of War, and was killed on July 10, 1916, fully deserved his decoration, for he had carried out many dangerous raids with rare skill and conspicuous bravery.

*   *   *

On July 5th, now in Humbercourt, miles away from the trenches, the Battalion received warning to move at short notice, and the same night, very late, we set out for the Somme. A fleet of buses stood waiting—good old London Generals—and into them we all clambered, with equipment and rifles and rations, and newly acquired tin hats. It was time now to say good-bye to trench warfare, at least for a season, and to reflect on the greater nightmare down in the South; but when someone asked, "Are we downhearted?" the whole bus-load roared a mighty "*No!*" The man near the door appointed himself conductor as the engine started to throb.

"Do you stop at the Savoy Hotel?" somebody asked him.

"No, sir!" came the quick reply. "Can't afford it! Did you say a tuppenny, sir, and one for the child? Comes cheaper if you take a return!"

LE GASTINEAU—AUXI—AND BACK AGAIN

We joked and laughed, as our bus charged into the night, with gears groaning each time we mounted a hill; and then after a lull, too nerve-racking to be endured for long, a fellow started a tune on a mouth-organ, and all the passengers joined lustily in the singing of "Mademoiselle from Armentieres," "Fred Karno's Army," "If you were the only girl in the world," "I want to go home!" "Who were you with last night?" and all those other songs in which British soldiers sought relief when threatened with attacks of nerves.

It was in this mood that men were going to the battle beyond, men mostly in the full bloom of youth, men who had joined up in 1914, some because they believed they were taking up a righteous cause, others in a sporting spirit as if war were only a game.

The hours of darkness were now speeding by, and one head after another began to nod as the bus rattled on and on. Presently a fair-haired lad stood up and shouted, "Look, boys, the dawn!" and out of the misty window, as we lurched round a corner, we saw to the East a cold, grey sky, overlaid with sullen clouds—clouds heavy with rain and a dark foreboding.

We were now reaching the end of our journey, the blood-bathed fields of the Somme.

CHAPTER V

THE TRAGIC SUMMER OF 1916

IT was July 6, 1916, and the Battle of the Somme was already in progress when we arrived that morning at Bresle, an uninviting village where we spent the remainder of the day. At five o'clock the same evening, now attached to the 19th Division, we set out for the line. We were soon marching up a steep bit of road, past a field battery halted for tea, and as we got to the top of the rise we saw long stretches of canvas fastened to plane-trees to hide the long procession of traffic from enemy observation; and then away to the North-East, the bursting of shells, till, after a time, we came to Albert, passing beneath the shattered cathedral tower from whose height the prone figure of the Virgin leaned sorrowfully over the town as if lamenting the folly of men. All that night, as we lay sleepless on the floors of deserted houses and shops, we listened to the rumble of limber wheels over cobbles and, in the distance, the endless drumming of guns.

Early next morning we were ordered to move forward, and after a hurried breakfast we started out for the Tara Usna ridge, about a mile up the Albert–Bapaume road. This was our position of assembly pending further instructions, and there we stood all day in the rain watching the extraordinary scene near the top of that ridge, which was like some vast crowded fair-ground, for to right and left, and behind, the landscape was dotted with bivouacs and dumps, horse-lines and batteries, cookers and watercarts, all mixed up with waiting infantry and gunners and cooks hard at work. Right in the midst of all this medley, French 75's were yapping like a million mad dogs, while the heavies added to the din, and British aeroplanes roared close overhead. As we watched, prisoners trudged by in large batches, all looking dirty and dazed; parties of wounded toiled slowly towards the dressing-stations, some limping along, others inert on stretchers, borne tenderly by Germans and Tommies alike; a demented British officer darted by, hatless, waving his arms, and shouting something that none of us understood; and then a shell burst on a dump to the left, sending up a great spout of flames and smoke and flying fragments. This, we realized, was the Battle of the Somme, and as day passed into evening we knew that some dreadful experience awaited us and thousands of others following on behind.

At ten o'clock that night we advanced to a new position. The track was over very difficult ground, and as we had to move along in single file our progress was painfully slow, but eventually after losing thirteen men killed or wounded by bursting shells, we reached the old British front line South of La Boiselle, with Contalmaison and Pozières lying out in the darkness beyond. There the Battalion kept garrison, with no sort of communication established with the units supposed to be on its flanks.

We remained in this position for two nights and two days, whilst our casualty list mounted steadily. Some success attended our efforts to strengthen these trenches, but there were other jobs to be done, worst among them the burial of the dead of the last nine days. There they were, poor devils, score upon score of the Tyneside Scottish, some with their rifles still wearing bolt-covers, so swiftly had death come to them. The great crater that yawned just in front of our line was made one vast tomb for these sturdy men from the North, but unfortunately the awful conditions prevented our burial parties from recovering the identity discs of the dead, and maybe some are still numbered among those who lie unnamed in the blood-drenched soil of France.

Whilst some of the flower of England's youth was lying out there in No Man's Land, newspapers arrived with our mail, newspapers emblazoned with headlines that told of

A GLORIOUS VICTORY ON THE SOMME!

Newspapers with pictures of laughing soldiers "waiting to go Over the Top." Masterpieces painted with a little printers' ink and a great deal of imagination!

On July 10th, a date memorable in the history of the 13th Rifle Brigade, we were in the front line as part of the 34th Division and the disposition of companies was:

"D" Company on the left of the tramway-line with "C" Company in support.

'A" Company on the right, with "B" Company in support.

Our position was heavily shelled during the day, and the casualty list grew in a few hours by another seventy killed or wounded.

At 8.15 that evening word was passed along that the Battalion would launch an attack on the German trenches in half an hour's time, and rum was issued to all the troops, now standing by with the chin-straps of their steel helmets pulled taut and gas-masks in the "alert." Men glanced at one another, and with a brave smile many tried hard to conceal their reaction to the dreadful ordeal just announced. A middle-aged chap would say to his pal, "Cheero, mate! Hope it's a blighty for both of us!" while a young, chubby-faced fellow would start to talk about something which had nothing to do with the War. . . .

At last, exactly at 8.45, the C.O.'s whistle gave the signal, the trench began to empty, and with "D" and "A" Companies leading the way, men were moving towards the German line just as they did at High Wycombe and on Salisbury Plain. Shells were bursting all round, the shrapnel descending like rain, the high explosive crashing and spouting up great black fountains of earth, while hidden machine-guns by the dozen poured out their pitiless streams of lead. The advancing lines of khaki were now being thinned at every yard, but the gaps filled up quickly and the dauntless survivors pressed on until at last they battered their way into the German front line; then, with the position won at a frightful cost, came the news that the assault was all a mistake. "Attack cancelled," said a message received by the Colonel, as he followed behind his men. So the order was given to retire, and all those who remained alive had to thread their way back again through a second inferno, over the dead, and over the wounded who had to be left behind.

Back now in the trench from which the attack had begun, small squads of men were closing up to answer a hurried roll-call. Gradually more men drifted in, and the number of survivors increased; but alas! the total was still appallingly small. Some days afterwards, when the casualty lists were made up and all the hospitals had rendered their reports, the losses were assessed at 20 officers and 380 other ranks. The C.O. and the Adjutant had been wounded, the Second-in-Command was missing, three of the Company Commanders had been killed, while the fourth was on his way to the C.C.S.; the Medical Officer was dead, Acting R.S.M. Croutcher severely wounded, and whole platoons of men had been completely wiped out.

The officers who took part in that valiant but fruitless adventure, from the Colonel down to the youngest Subaltern, were greatly admired by their men, and no unit of the British Army ever had a better conception of discipline, or a more profound experience of comradeship. It can be said truthfully of the officers who went into action on the Somme with the 13th Rifle Brigade, that they were all soldiers and gentlemen, and those who died in the attack of July 10th will be remembered with affection till the last of the riflemen who went Over the Top on that fateful evening has himself been dismissed from Life's last parade. The death of such men as Major Sir Foster Cunliffe and Capt. G. W. Smith was a severe blow to the world of learning as well as to the Battalion, for both had been distinguished scholars. Before the War, Capt. Smith was lecturer in the Department of Zoology and

Comparative Anatomy at Oxford, and his monographs dealing with his research expeditions to the Antipodes gained for him a permanent place in the records of Natural Science. Sir Foster Cunliffe's diary, containing his last thoughts as he lay slowly dying in a shell-hole, was probably the most moving document ever recovered from the battlefield—almost as beautiful and poignant in its phrasing as Scott's final message from the South Pole.

When the Battalion had returned from its terrible experience there came to the mind of each survivor a cynical and lasting impression of the true significance of modern warfare. Men stood in little groups, brooding on the tragedy and caring not what happened next. Many still wore an ashen-grey look, their eyes revealing a half-demented mind. More than one was pondering on the fate of a loved brother, perhaps still alive out there in some ditch filled with dead comrades.

Col. Pretor-Pinney, although wounded, remained in command until the last of the stragglers came in, when he reluctantly agreed to go back to the big dressing-station down in the town of Albert. There he remained for a time, a pathetic figure, that habitual calm of his changed into unchecked emotion, as with tears streaming down his face he kept repeating, "What a mess they've made of my Battalion!" Ever since 1914 he had watched the 13th Rifle Brigade steadily developing into a body of troops after the pattern of his days in the Regular Army, and his pride in their perfection was the greatest thing in his life. Behind his soldierly restraint he really loved his men, and the sacrifice of so many young lives in a futile operation ordered and then cancelled too late was to him the very abyss of calamity.

On the morning of July 11th the remnant of the Battalion was relieved by the 10th R.F., and then retired to the third line. At intervals during the day the enemy bombarded our new position and the casualty list, already a ghastly length, kept on growing hour after hour until 11 p.m., when we moved back to the trenches which had been the enemy's second line up to the opening of the Somme Battle. Next day our gradual withdrawal from the firing line was continued, and we proceeded to the Tara Usna system of trenches, where we remained for a couple of days. It was here, at Hampstead Heath (a place very unlike London's playground of that name), that two of "C" Company's cooks were killed by a 5·9. Another man about the same time had an ankle broken by the base of a shell which blew back some 200 yards after the burst. On July 17th, now in the old German support line, Lieut.-Col. D. E. Prideaux-Brune became Commanding Officer, and Major O. B. Graham, also from a Regular Battalion of the Rifle Brigade, was appointed Second-in-Command.

Two days afterwards we came out of the trenches and stayed the first night at Albert. Although reinforced by two large drafts the Thirteenth looked but a shadow of its old self, and during the dreary march back to Bresle next morning, there were many who were thinking sadly of comrades no longer with that magnificent Battalion which had travelled eastwards along the same road only a fortnight before. Even the newly joined men were silent, and no one wanted to sing when marching easy. The new C.O. seemed to know how we felt, for when C.S.M. Keene, now acting as R.S.M., gave the order "March to Attention," Col. Prideaux-Brune immediately said, with a wave of the hand, "Cut it out, Sergeant-Major, and the men can smoke if they like." How vivid that small highlight of pity seemed against the black despair which had been possessing our minds.

We had ten days in the dirty village of Bresle, making up our lost equipment, and getting the recruits into shape. New officers now joined, but our complement was only up to twelve, including the C.O., the Second-in-Command and the Transport Officer, when we returned to the trenches on July 30th.

We first of all occupied the Support line, between Bottom Wood and Shelter Wood, with field-guns just behind jolting our jaded nerves day and night and the stench of half-buried dead in our nostrils. After a bit we moved forward to a position just South of Mametz Wood, where we were heavily shelled on the night of August 6th, losing 21 killed and 23 wounded. Most of the dead were original members of the Battalion and wonderful comrades, among them poor Starbuck, Corporal of the snipers, a good-looking Somerset lad who had a cheery smile for everyone and such bright mischievous eyes. Earlier the same day nearly all the men killed had filled up some funk-holes in their trench, on instructions from a certain Staff Officer who was making an infrequent visit to the line, and the only one who escaped death in that trench on that horrible night was a fellow lying in his funk-hole who had defied the official command. Many were the tragedies enacted in the years of the War merely to satisfy the personal whims of people who wore red-banded hats.

On August 8th we went forward again, this time to the Support line South-East of Bazentin-le-Petit, Battalion Headquarters being accommodated in a chalk-pit next to the village cemetery. Every now and then the Germans plastered that chalk-pit with shells, and many fine fellows perished there, including Corpl. Tice of the Pioneers, whose only brother had been killed in the useless attack of July 10th.

After spending three days in the Support line and another period in the Reserve trenches, we went back once more to our verminous barns in the village of Bresle.

*   *   *

Our nightmare on the Somme now over, we boarded the train at Frechicourt on August 18th, and arrived at Citerne the same evening. From there, at midnight, motor lorries took us to Lampré, where we started another railway journey, and then came two days in billets in the pleasant little town of Estaires, followed by another trip in horse-wagons as far as Ourton.

Back again in the good old 37th Division, we left Ourton and marched to Verdrel, where we had eleven days of well-deserved rest. We were now in a northern coal-mining area, and after spending a night at Fosse 10, we came to Calonne and took over the village defence line. A few days later we moved into the front line. The trenches here ran in and out of the abandoned houses and it was a new experience to descend from the firestep straight into a front parlour still boasting a table and chairs and various things gathered from other rooms. In most of these dwellings the period of usefulness of some of the contents had long ago been ended by a series of enemy bombardments, and in one house the choice of serviceable things was so limited that the soldier occupants had to wash themselves in a bedroom utensil not normally used for that purpose. What would the French housewife have said, they wondered, had she been able to revisit the old home when half-stripped Tommies were performing their morning ablutions? But they agreed that in all probability Madame would merely have shrugged her shoulders and declared "*Ça ne fait rien! C'est la guerre!*"

For about a month we shared with the 13th R.F. the job of holding the line East of Calonne, where the view embraced a number of dismal coaltips, and, farther off, the town of Lens. It was a mining area all right, even in those days, for the earth was burrowed and mined by tunnelling Companies on both sides, and as if to enlarge our interest in a war that was growing more modern every day, displays were frequently given by trench mortars and rifle grenades. The *minenwerfer* shells sent over by old Jerry could be seen in flight, and it paid us to try and dodge them, as on landing they usually made a terrible mess. It was this type of missile which severely wounded Capt. G. G. Rivière on September 26th. He was the last of the Company officers who joined the Battalion in 1914 and immensely popular.

On coming out of the line at the end of each tour of duty, a march of less than two miles would bring us to the village of Bully-Grenay, where little shops still did business, and where a woman barber cut our hair for a fee hardly more than that which we usually paid for a gaol-bird crop, at the hands of comrades whose connection with the hair-dressing trade had begun in the Army.

* * *

After a short period in the trenches in front of Maroc—another mining place, but much more attractive than Calonne—we left this sector and on October 17th set out again for the South. Marching via Barlin, La Thieuloye, Houvin-Houvigneuil, Doullens and Gezaincourt, we came to Puchevillers, and in that dreary village we started to practise the attack. Another big offensive was in the offing, and we soon knew that we were going to take part in it; but with the rain coming down every day and conditions growing steadily worse in the area of the projected attack, the plans of the High Command had to be postponed, so we took a westerly route once more.

During the long day's march to our new destination, rain poured down without ceasing until the late afternoon, when the weather suddenly

THE TRAGIC SUMMER OF 1916

improved, and it was then, as we halted at the side of the road for the usual hourly rest, that we saw in the sky a picture of exquisite beauty. In the West, on a little hill, stood a lovely old windmill, its dark motionless sails stretched out in perfect silhouette against a backcloth on which had been painted a dark-red sun, with wisps of cloud all mauve and orange and grey. There was not a man amongst us who did not "stand and stare."

Darkness had set in when we reached the village of Longuevillette, where on the following day we began in real earnest to rehearse the big drama for which we had been withdrawn from our tour in the North. On training-ground marked out with long lines of white tape, groups of Riflemen practised the attack, while, on a site not far away, the bombers hurled small cast-iron pineapples and the Lewis gunners rattled off drum after drum of S.A.A. Still, there were other things to claim our attention such as sports, football and concerts—all designed by the officers to keep us fit and to divert our minds from the grim business of war. As a *grand finale*, on the last Sunday afternoon of our stay in this charming spot, there was a Rugby match—The Officers versus The Rest—and great was the excitement on the touch-lines as first one side and then the other took the lead. Towards the end of the game, when the struggle grew fast and furious, Col. Prideaux-Brune fell heavily and broke his collar-bone in tackling a robust little Sergeant who was going all out for a try. In less than four months he had become very popular, and when he left us that evening, in an ambulance car, a huge crowd of the boys gathered round. We all felt that we had lost a C.O. who was also a friend.

On the morning of November 11th, with Major O. B. Graham now in command, the Battalion marched away from Longuevillette. Soon after that long day's trek had begun, we found that two handsome goats had tacked themselves on to the usual procession of dogs, and during our first halt it occurred to Sergt. Stott that goat's milk was just the stuff to give the troops. So mess-tins were quickly unfastened and each of the lads nearby received an ample ration of rich creamy milk.

In the evening we came once more to Puchevillers, that dirty inhospitable village at which we had stayed less than a fortnight before, where liquid mud streamed over the roads, where most of the wells were padlocked, and where biscuits and chocolate were sold in the shops at grossly inflated prices. It was here, in these dismal surroundings, that the Battalion had a quick final preparation for the coming ordeal of winter and death in the Valley of the Ancre.

Lt.-Col. D. E. PRIDEAUX-BRUNE, D.S.O.
Commanding the Battalion from July to November 1916.

CHAPTER VI

THE BATTLE OF THE ANCRE

ON November 12, 1916, we moved on to Hedauville, and spent the night there in bivouacs. Next morning we continued our march to the trenches, and after resting awhile near Englebelmer we pushed on to Mesnil and Hamel; then, late the same night, we trudged our way to the Green Line, our appointed place of assembly for the pending Battle of the Ancre. During the last stage of this dreary journey in the rain and the sleet, our route was heavily shelled and we lost many splendid fellows, including Sergt.-Major Williams, of "C" Company, hero of many a fight, mentioned in despatches and awarded a posthumous Military Medal. Illtyd Williams had great personal charm as well as magnificent courage, and above all he was a wonderful pal.

At 4.15 on the morning of November 14th the Battalion had warning to launch an attack on the German trenches in two hours' time. The objective was Beaucourt Trench, and the 13th R.F. were to be on our left, with the H.A.C. (63rd Division) on our right. The assault was held up by heavy rifle and machine-gun fire for close on an hour, but the Battalion went forward at 7.15 under cover of a protecting barrage from our Artillery, and after a terrific struggle gained a firm footing in the enemy's defences some three hundred yards North-West of Railway Alley, capturing large batches of prisoners and huge quantities of material. Our left flank had now become exposed and enemy snipers were giving a lot of trouble, but after a time the newly won position was finally consolidated and our bombers then started blasting their way up Beaucourt Trench towards Leave Avenue. By midnight more ground had been wrested from the Germans, and on the following day the men of "D" Company rounded off the Battalion's success by taking Muck Trench. It was in this final onslaught that Sergt.-Major Oliver, singlehanded, frightened twenty-three of the enemy into surrender, although his only means of defence at that time were just one Mills bomb and an empty revolver. This brave old veteran of past campaigns seemed completely oblivious to personal danger, and no one was surprised to hear on the morning after the capture of Muck Trench that his batman had found him on the top step of a dug-out full of Germans, reading a letter which he had received from home just before going into action.

The Battle of the Ancre, fought in wintry conditions of the worst kind, was proclaimed a military success, yet our rejoicing was on a muted note for once again our losses were appalling. Included in the 93 dead were 2nd Lieut. W. D. M. Wilkinson, Coy. Sergt.-Majors Williams, James and Squires, and Sergts. Dean, Green, Harris, Martyr, Tomkinson and Wally, while there were eleven officers on the wounded list, among them Capt. T. G. Skyrme, a South African, Lieut. R. Colvill-Jones from Buenos Aires, and Capt. Colin Gilray, a New Zealander once famous on the Rugby field. Battalion Headquarters went through a very bad time, losing nearly all the runners and most of the aid-post staff. With deep regret we learned that the gentle-hearted chaplain, the Rev. E. W. Trevor, had died a hero's death while helping to succour the wounded in a dressing station at Hamel.

*   *   *

We were relieved by the 10th R.F. on the night of November 15th, and after spending another five days in the Green Line, followed by one night in bivouacs at Englebelmer, we marched to Louvencourt, where we found letters and parcels from home, the first for nearly a fortnight. The next move was to Puchevillers, that village which none of us loved, and there we stayed for sixteen days. Lieut.-Col. F. S. N. Savage-Armstrong now took command of the

Battalion, and on December 13th we set out for another part of the Front through Authiele, Nœux, Œuf, Beauvois, Heuchin, Auchy-au-Bois, Calonne-sur-la-Lys and Paradis. After eight days of marching we reached Croix Barbée, a deserted village just a mile or so behind the trenches of Neuve Chapelle. When the 12th Gloucesters handed over their billets they told us that Croix Barbée was a "cushy" spot—"jam on it!" they said—and there was nothing to disturb our sense of security until the evening of December 24th, when we had a Christmas-box from the enemy. For a whole hour we sat in a downpour of lachrymatory gas shells, and death seemed very near as first one flash, then another, would light up our bare rooms, the gas penetrating under our goggles and giving us acute pain in the eyes. When at last the storm ended no one wanted to resume the singing of carols—it seemed so incongruous to chant the old Christmas hymns with men lying dead and no sign of good will. Many who died on that Christmas Eve had been rehearsing the carols and songs they had proposed to sing the next day, among them Robinson, that likeable chap who was Bombing Sergeant attached to Battalion Headquarters.

With the cloud of recent tragedy not yet lifted, Christmas Day passed quietly, and shortly afterwards the Battalion went into the front line, a system of defences consisting mainly of breastworks, with a series of sentry posts connected up with barbed wire. That flat country round Neuve Chapelle was all ditches and dykes, and in many places the wire entanglements were only just visible above the slimy water.

On completing our first tour of the line in this sector, we started a period of rest and training, and as we could not all be accommodated in one spot, billets had to be found for us in a widely scattered area, which included the villages of Paradis, La Coutre and Vielle Chapelle —all pleasant places where the kindly peasants helped us to establish contact once again with long-lost civilization.

At the end of a fortnight, soon after receiving a visit from the Corps Commander, who came along to present medal-ribbons to those who had gained distinction on the Somme, we moved up again to Croix Barbée, where we remained for a week, sending working parties up to the forward area every night and morning. We then took over the front line from the 13th R.F., and almost as soon as the relief operation had been completed, we lost seven killed and one wounded through the blowing up of a Stokes Mortar ammunition dump, hit by a German shell. With the rain coming down in a ceaseless torrent every day and increased attention from the enemy's *minenwerfer*, life became none too happy in the Neuve Chapelle sector, so it was a glad message that brought us news of another move.

*   *   *

On January 27, 1917, we marched to La Fosse, where we remained for the rest of that month. During our stay, the Army Commander, Gen. Sir H. S. Horne, K.C.B., held a review at Merville, and complimented the Battalion's guard of honour on their smart and soldierly appearance. At this parade some more of our fellows were decorated for their bravery in the Battles of the Somme and the Ancre. Col. D. E. Prideaux-Brune was now back, but he left us again in a few days to take command of another unit.

We left La Fosse on February 1st, and went into G.H.Q. Reserve at Robermetz, a pleasant village not far away, and then a fortnight later, staying en route at Bethune and Philosophe, we marched to the trenches in the Hulluch Left sector. Here we spent three weeks, part of the time in the front line and the remainder in the Support line, while old Jerry kept on sending us his kind regards in many different forms, including "minnies," "flying pigs," rifle-grenades and aerial darts. The soil in these trenches was mainly soft chalk, and it was hard work shovelling back the little bits of the parapet that fell into the trench following the concussion of each bombardment. The trouble known as Trench Feet now appeared, and the number thus lost to the Battalion kept on growing steadily in spite of all the rigid precautions and a panicky note from Divisional Headquarters indicating that someone back there was beginning to feel "the wind in the vertical."

It was in the Hulluch sector that Bill Gregg started his brilliant collection of war decorations. A dead German lay out in a deep crater between the opposing lines, and the decree had gone forth that his identification must be obtained, although it would of course be a risky business with an enemy sentry looking over the lip of that crater at irregular intervals. But Gregg, then just a plain Rifleman, who knew no fear, volunteered for the job, and crawling down into that hole on a bright spring morning, spent a long time searching the decomposed body, keeping one eye on the enemy sentry-post all the while. His luck was in, and he managed to get back unharmed, with a complete outfit of German shoulder-straps, identity disc, paybook and letters. All his chums thought that he fully deserved the M.M. awarded to him for his daring on that occasion, but none even dreamed that, within the next fifteen months, this brave fellow from Heanor would also win the V.C. and the D.C.M.

We came out of the line in the early morning of March 1st, and after slithering down the communication trench, waterlogged and measuring close on a mile, we arrived at Mazingarbe, and from there on the following day marched to Chocques. We then went to Fontes, where Col. Savage-Armstrong gave up the command of the Battalion to Col. Pretor-Pinney, now recovered from his wound in the Somme Battle, and obviously glad to be back among his men.

* * *

On March 10th we moved to Mesnil St. Pol, where we soon became aware that the Battalion was due for another big scrap. Day after day armed parties stormed over marked-out training-ground, and bombers and Lewis gunners added their quota to the din which had now disturbed the peace of this remote village, while the Quartermaster-Sergeants were keeping themselves busy making up deficiencies in kit and equipment.

Our long preparation for the coming ordeal ended on the morning of April 5th, when we marched to Villers-sur-Simon, and next day we tramped to Agnez-les-Duisans, where we rested for the night in grubby hutments lying among a small group of desolate trees. On the following morning we continued our march forward, until, when darkness came, we found ourselves on the outskirts of Wagonlieu.

One by one the candles went out in the low-roofed bivouacs, as tired soldiers stretched themselves on waterproof sheets and pulled their greatcoats over their heads, hoping to find sleep and forgetfulness before the curtain went up on the morrow.

CHAPTER VII

THE BATTLE OF ARRAS 1917

WE awoke to a perfect spring morning. It was April 9, 1917. On a grassy hill under the blue dome of the sky, with aeroplanes glistening overhead in the sun, a small company of us gathered round Col. Pretor-Pinney and the white-surpliced padre, for the service of Holy Communion, a last solemn Easter celebration before going into action.

Soon afterwards, the C.O. gave the order to move and we started on the last stage of our march to the battle line. After resting for a time near Fred's Wood, North of Arras, we made our way under heavy shelling to the Brown Line, and at eight o'clock that night hurried forward to assist the 13th R.F., who were going through a bad time on the Feuchy-Chapelle road.

At four o'clock the next morning instructions were received to march at once to a point near Broken Hill, and the move was carried out successfully. Later, we were warned to be ready to take up a more advanced position, but at 5 p.m. the order was cancelled as the 10th R.F. and the 13th R.F. had been compelled to fall back some three hundred yards and dig themselves in, so the assault was postponed.

Early on April 11th, long before it was light, the Brigadier gave verbally to Battalion Commanders the details of an attack which had been arranged for five o'clock that morning. The 13th Rifle Brigade were to form the left of the attacking force, with the 13th K.R.R.C. on the right and the two Fusilier Battalions in support.

The last traces of night were still in the sky when the advance began. With the two leading Companies in two waves, the other Companies behind in similar formation, and four Lewis guns to protect the exposed left flank, the Rifle Brigade darted forward through a storm of shells and machine-gun bullets, which soon began to make big gaps in the advancing files of men. Wavering, but quickly recovering, the survivors charged over the fire-swept ground, and then up the long slope which led to the village of Monchy-le-Preux, a slope which had defied the heroic endeavours of many other Battalions of British Infantry since Easter Monday morning. Now fighting every yard desperately, madly, the men of the Thirteenth gradually drew near their objective until at last that bloody height was theirs, along with the village stronghold which the enemy had been ordered to hold at all costs. It was here at Monchy-le-Preux that a memorial was raised after the War to the dead of our Division. It was here too that we saw the cavalry in action—a glorious but futile charge by the 2nd Dragoons who got as far as the village only to be caught, horses and men, in a holocaust of bursting shells. To see those beautiful steeds galloping back riderless, some wounded beyond all hope, was a pitiful sight.

At 10.30 that night the Battalion was relieved and went from the scene of its hard-won victory, first of all to the Brown Line and, a few hours later, to Battery Valley. Next morning we marched into Arras, most of us finding accommodation in the vast cellars of the Grande Place, each cellar big enough to take a whole Platoon.

Orders arrived from Brigade soon after midnight and were duly despatched from the Orderly Room to the Acting Adjutant; but about an hour later the runners returned to report that they could not find his billet, whereupon the Orderly Room Sergeant, sleepless and furious, himself embarked on a tour of the darkened streets of the city. But he, too, failed to get into touch with the Acting Adjutant, so, with dawn fast approaching, he went back to the Grande Place, and after opening the Brigade message, which said that the Battalion would move at 6.30 a.m., he decided to give his own written directions to the Company Commanders, thus assuming powers not compatible with his lowly rank. However, this breach of "good order and military discipline" was cheerfully overlooked by the Colonel when he learned what had happened and saw all the troops on parade at the appointed hour, ready to board the waiting lorries.

After a short period of rest and training at Agnez-les-Duisans and Villers-sur-Simon, we returned to the battle-front, relieving the 1st Rifle Brigade in the support trenches at Blangy. There were traps for the unwary in some of the dug-outs, laid there by Jerry just before he decided to give up this bit of the line, and one of our officers got a nasty wound when he pulled an innocent-looking wire which had been attached to a hidden stick-bomb.

We were now due for another venture Over the Top, this time in the neighbourhood of Gavrelle, where the second phase of the Battle of Arras was fiercely proceeding, and very early on the morning of April 23rd we stood waiting for the signal to advance. When zero hour arrived (4.45 a.m.), the leading waves of the attacking force moved out in artillery formation, just as the enemy was putting down a heavy barrage of 5·9 H.E. shells. The advance, only temporarily checked, was continued with amazing vigour in spite of rapidly increasing casualties, and the objective was gained after some ruthless hand-to-hand fighting. The enemy, crushed for the moment, now decided on a counter-attack; but before his bombers could get into their stride, they met a bombing party in charge of 2nd Lieut. W. M. Smith. A terrific struggle took place, ending in the surrender of all the surviving Germans.

Soon after the advance began, Col. Pretor-Pinney was mortally wounded, and while Capt. the Hon. R. W. Morgan-Grenville was on his way to Battalion Headquarters to take command, he, too, was severely wounded. Capt. C. N. C. Boyle then took charge. At the end of the first spell of fighting that morning most of the survivors were in the Black Line trying to dodge the shells now tearing down on them with increasing force.

Major A. N. Strode Jackson took over the command of the Battalion at 9 a.m., just as efforts were being made to determine what force was still available for the next phase of the attack. The casualties had been frightfully heavy, and at a quick estimate there were not more than four officers and 120 men left. A little later the effective strength was slightly increased by the return of a small group of Riflemen who had got mixed up with the 63rd Division, but the number of survivors was still very small. Among those evacuated to the casualty clearing stations

THE BATTLE OF ARRAS 1917

that morning was C.S.M. Tarlton. He was carrying a pocketful of Verey lights and aeroplane flares as he moved off to the attack, when a bursting shell set them alight. It was a strange sight to see a Sergeant-Major rolling on the ground, but with one arm rendered useless he could do little else, and he had a desperate time really in trying to end the firework display. Poor Tarlton, badly hurt, did not want to go down with colours flying in this fashion, and when he recovered consciousness as he lay back on a stretcher carried by four Jerries, it was characteristic of him that he should be thinking of his Company and wondering how they were faring without their ration of rockets.

Later in the day, the remnant of the Battalion carried the attack a stage further, and in collaboration with the 13th K.R.R.C. a strong defence line was established in a sunken road. The K.R.R.'s now reported that they were being enfiladed by German snipers, so we sent out a party to protect their flank. At 5.30 p.m. news came through that a large enemy force was in a commanding position within sixty yards of us, and that the Lewis gunners defending our right posts had been knocked out, so Capt.Boyle and his men went out in skirmishing order to deal with the situation, and after a time they succeeded in straightening out the line.

In the early hours of April 24th three of our reserve Lewis gun teams reported at Battalion Headquarters in the sunken road, having lost their direction in the first onslaught on the previous day and gone Over the Top with the men of the 63rd Division in their valiant but fruitless attack on the village of Gavrelle.

On April 25th we heard that the operations carried out by the 63rd and the 112th Infantry Brigades had been unsuccessful, so on the following day we received orders to be ready to resume the offensive. Major A. N. Strode Jackson, although wounded, remained in charge of the Battalion until 9.30 that night, when Lieut.-Col. W. R. Stewart, M.C., became our Commanding Officer, and the Battalion was in Cuba trench all the next day. Notwithstanding their trying experiences during the past week the troops were in remarkably good fettle.

The attack launched early the next morning, April 28th, brilliantly planned by our new C.O., was a complete success, and in less than two hours we were in possession of our objective, with the enemy completely routed. Nearly all the prisoners taken were huge Bavarians, and it made us all laugh to see about twenty of them marching away in charge of a Corporal who was only five-foot-one in his socks. To make sure that none would run away, he had made every

LT.-COL. W. R. STEWART, D.S.O., M.C.

Commanding the Battalion from April 1917 until killed in action on April 8, 1918.

THE BATTLE OF ARRAS 1917

man surrender his trouser-belt, so that each of the poor devils had to keep his hands in his pockets to avoid catastrophe.

* * *

The Battalion achieved fame in the Battle of Arras. Monchy was won on April 11th, and the operations carried out near Gavrelle from April 23rd to April 28th were regarded by the High Command as entirely successful. But against the glory of victory must be set the tragedy of the Casualty Lists. The dead alone numbered more than 130, including a great many who had been with the Battalion since 1914, and such gallant young officers as Capt. J. W. Bowyer and 2nd Lieuts. G. B. Bagnall, W. E. Hobday, A. I. Rae, W. L. T. Rhys and J. W. Spanton, as well as the Grand Old Man of the Battalion, Lieut.-Col. C. F. Pretor-Pinney, D.S.O., who died of wounds received in the Gavrelle offensive. Our first Commanding Officer, an admired and respected leader, this fine soldier went Over the Top on the morning of April 23rd carrying only cane and gloves. Shells were bursting round him, as, cool and imperturbable as ever, with a wave of the hand as if directing a practice movement, he led the advancing troops towards the enemy's lines.

Unhappily he was soon hit by a fragment of shell, and when the stretcher-bearers carried him gently away, it seemed that he had little chance of recovery. He died at a Casualty Clearing Station on April 28th, at the age of fifty-two, and was buried at Aubigny.

*   *   *

From May 1st to May 17th we were at Villers-sur-Simon where, in the intervals of training, we tried to forget the War by organizing concerts, sports and inter-Company football matches. We even managed to find humour here and there. For instance, the little Corporal who had so convulsed us by pinching the belts of his squad of prisoners, had also acquired from them a large assortment of watches, cigarette cases and pocket-knives. With the money obtained from the sale of these souvenirs he got so gloriously tight that, when the Battalion was ready to move off, we had to hide him in the blanket lorry to save him from arrest and a Field General Court Martial.

Then there was the Corporal-cook of "A" Company, who, deciding that his Company badly needed fresh vegetables, cast covetous eyes on a field of carrots and turnips and cabbages. A past-master in the gentle art of scrounging, and inspired by the pathetic appeal on the tailboards of lorries,

WHAT HAVE YOU SALVED TO-DAY?

he went out in the dead of night with a number of helpers, each armed with sacks, and soon collected plenty of tasty substitutes for the Army lime-juice. The Corporal secured the vegetables, but the Battalion got the bill. . . .

* * *

On May 19th we went back to the line, and, after one night in Schramm Barracks in Arras and a period of duty in the Reserve trenches East of Tilloy, we went into the front line in the Monchy-Guemappe Sector, where the enemy, entrenched in a system of shell-holes, provided our snipers with a lot of shooting practice. At 11.30 p.m. on May 30th, following orders from Brigade to carry out a demonstration in conjunction with the 29th Division who were on our left, we sent out three attacking parties; but on reaching the German wire one of these found the enemy quite prepared, so with no artillery support, the whole of our attacking force was reluctantly compelled to withdraw. The next day's *Comic Cuts*—the official news summary—referred to the venture as a "Minor Operation," yet the Battalion lost 54 killed or wounded. Among the dead was 2nd Lieut. F. B. Johnson. On the following night, just before we left again for the Reserve trenches, 2nd Lieut. R. O. Bassham was killed, exactly a month after joining the Battalion.

We marched back to Arras on June 2nd, and boarded motor lorries bound for Berlencourt. A few days later we had another lorry-ride to Sachin, and from there marched to Erny St. Julien, a charming village where we hoped to enjoy a period of peace and relaxation; but though out of sound of the guns we still had the eternal "training for the Attack," which seemed to us rather an unnecessary occupation for troops who had recently been Over the Top three times in three weeks. However, things were not bad on the whole, for the play spirit was encouraged in every way by Col. Stewart and the other officers, and there was a programme of concerts, football and sports ending with a "Grand Athletic Meeting" at which we had our first glimpse of Major A. N. Strode Jackson on the running-track. He had entered for the Mile Handicap, but did not appear to take the race seriously until the bell sounded for the last lap, when he got into a raking stride and covered the ground in a way which gave us an idea of his record performance in the Olympic Games at Stockholm. This famous Oxford athlete reached the tape first, yet, like the good sport he was, he allowed the first prize to go to a little Welshman with plenty of pluck but much shorter legs.

Our respite from the battle area seemed too good to last, and on June 23rd we had to leave this green valley for the desolate plains of Flanders.

CHAPTER VIII

THE YPRES SALIENT

STOPPING one night at Guarbecque we marched to La Kruele, two kilos North of Hazebrouck, and arrived there on June 24, 1917. We were now in the Second Army and on the following day we occupied a camp near Locre, moving a few nights later to the Support line on the far side of the Messines Ridge, the scene of a recent British success. Battalion Headquarters was at Torreken Farm, overlooked by German observation balloons. A little way behind was the village of Wytschaete, where, in a cellar, the Y.M.C.A. traded in cups of tea, biscuits and chocolate—the first time for us to see the sign of the Red Triangle so near to the trenches.

Our duties as Support Battalion included day and night work under the supervision of the Royal Engineers. It was often dangerous work, and one very dark night one of our digging parties was almost wiped out by a salvo of enemy shells.

After six days in the front line we marched to hutments at Dranoutre, and continued to supply fatigue parties to such an extent that the real function of the Infantry seemed to be getting more obscure every day. With the knowledge that the R.E.'s drew much better pay, our fellows often delighted in singing an appropriate song on their way back from their navvying, laying special emphasis on the words:

> The more we work, the more we may,
> It makes no difference to our pay.

On completing our next tour of duty in the line we came back to Lightning Farm and Beaver Hall on Kemmel Hill—the place where the Kaiser held a grand review of his troops during the following May.

On August 1st, a date which prompted dreams of holidays in the misty past, we were back in the Wytschaete sector, going up the next day to the Ridge Defence Line, with Battalion Headquarters at Lumm Farm and outposts North of Rifle Farm. While here a selected crowd of our fellows launched a night raid. The affair was most successful and old Jerry got a hammering, though we had a number of wounded, among them Lieut. E. Walpole, who was awarded the M.C. for leading the adventure, and that cheerful lad O'Connor, who received a bar to his M.M.

We came out of the line at the end of a week, and the day after we reached our old encampment on Kemmel Hill, news went round that four of the Battalion's bicycles were missing.

Corpl. Roff of the runners said that they must have perished during the last bombardment, but the Orderly Room Sergeant replied that explanations were no good at all to the people at Headquarters, adding that the establishment of nine bicycles would have to be made up immediately as the Strength Return was already due at Brigade.

"Don't worry, Serg.!" said the Corporal. "We'll get them bikes replaced toot sweet."

Gathering his boys about him, he told them of a plan. An hour later they all turned up at the pioneers' shop with four first-rate machines, purloined, at a favourable moment, from an R.E. dump down the road. It did not take them long to transform those bicycles completely, to paint out the R.E. sign and substitute the R.B.'s nicely camouflaged with dirt, and to exchange parts, here and there, with others from the Battalion's own machines. When the Engineer-Sergeant called next day in quest of four bicycles which had mysteriously disappeared, he was allowed to inspect each of our nine machines, but he went away completely satisfied that he had done us a wrong in doubting our honesty. For a change, the R.B.'s had "got one in" on the R.E.'s. It was worth a hundred digging parties.

From Kemmel we moved to Birr Barracks, a collection of huts near the village of Locre,

THE YPRES SALIENT

the Officers' Mess being housed in the Convent School of St. Anthony. Apart from providing fatigues and carrying out the inevitable training, we kept out of touch with the business of war during the next fortnight, although our minds were brought back to it again when we were asked to attend the funeral of Brig.-Gen. R. C. Maclachlan, D.S.O., Commander of the 112th Infantry Brigade, who had been killed in the trenches. As he was a distinguished soldier of the Rifle Brigade, it was fitting that the bearers and firing-party at his burial should come from a Battalion of the Green Jackets.

The Birthday of the Regiment was celebrated on August 25th, when bands from Divisional Headquarters and the 8th Somersets enlivened the programme of sports and football. Unfortunately we lost to the Australians at Rugby, our first defeat since arriving in France, but it would probably have been a victory for the R.B.'s had we been able to keep that wonderful team which we had before the Somme, then composed almost entirely of South Africans, with a sprinkling of Welshmen.

After Locre came the Reserve trenches in Rossignol Wood, and then the front line in Denys Wood. The rainy season had now set in, and with the trenches in a bad condition, the dugouts all lousy and damp, and hot food scarcely obtainable, there was very little comfort to be had. During our period of duty here (on August 29th) we lost Capt. H. N. Ries, who was badly wounded by a shell and incapacitated for the rest of the War. This popular young officer had been acting as Adjutant for the last four months.

On being relieved we went back a little way, to Irish House, but we did not stay there very long, for we soon went up to the trenches at Spoil Bank. The weather was now getting steadily worse, and our trips to the line and back were so frequent that we laughed heartily when one of the boys said: "I know what they'll call us if we get much more of this—the Umbrella Battalion, always up and down!" During the next twenty-four days we rested in a camp at Beaver Corner, manned the trenches alongside the Ypres–Comines Canal, stayed in another camp called Wakefield Huts, went up again to the front line, returned to Willibeke Camp, and finally reached the Support line in the Mont Sorrel Sector. In the meantime our casualty list was mounting up, and each tour of the trenches ended with forty to fifty killed or wounded. Among the dead were 2nd Lieut. E. McD. Campbell, killed five weeks after joining the Battalion, and C.S.M. Nethercott, who had been with us since 1914, a fellow with bright auburn hair, a cheerful disposition and a great capacity for comradeship. We also lost Major A. N. Strode Jackson, D.S.O., one of the few remaining officers of the old Battalion, who left us to take command of the 13th K.R.R.C. Included in the reinforcements continually arriving about this time was dear old Paddy Miles, our eighth and last R.S.M.

Leaving the Mont Sorrel trenches we marched to a camp, curiously named Dead Dog Farm. During our stay here a small group of Riflemen who had been lucky enough to remain together since September 1914 received a visit one night from an old comrade now in the Tanks. What a time they had together, recalling the good old days at Winchester and High Wycombe! Presently the arrival of the rum ration provoked so wistful a look on the face of the visitor, and so pathetic a plea that rum was rarely issued in the Tank Corps, that his hosts pressed upon him their combined issue, till his merry face shone brighter than ever and his laugh nearly lifted the rickety corrugated roof. He left in the early morning, somewhat sobered, but loudly testifying to the splendid qualities of the 13th R.B.'s.

After a short stay at Locrehof Farm we made a journey in motor lorries to St. Jean, not very far from Ypres, and there we resumed a life under canvas, a type of shelter that was of little use with enemy aircraft frequently flying overhead and dropping bombs near by. The escapes we had were really miraculous, and the worst thing that happened was the midnight arrival of a small "egg" in the Quartermaster's stores, which merely scattered a few tins of Ideal Milk, and caused Harry Rockall, the grey-haired storeman, to let loose a storm of abuse.

On October 29th we had another trip in motor lorries, this time to Strazeele, well behind Bailleul and Meteren. Here we were again in rural scenes, though it was still a Flanders landscape, flat, hedgeless country, with only an occasional poplar or church tower to relieve the monotony. However, Col. Stewart was all for stimulating his men to forget the War, and he inspired all kinds of distractions, including the Battalion Sports, held towards the end of our stay. At these Sports "D" Company got first place for drill and "B" Company won the Yukon Pack competition, but the outstanding event, the cross-country race, was won by Sergt. Gregg, then the holder of the D.C.M. and M.M. All the other entrants, over 400 officers and men, finished this race in the allotted time, so proving their astonishing fitness in spite of their rough time in the trenches.

On leaving Strazeele we journeyed to Kemmel Shelters, and later to a position North-East of Klein Zillebeke, where the front-line defences consisted of a series of shell-holes, and where sniping was the chief occupation on both sides. All the people belonging to Battalion Headquarters were in a pill-box, once used by the enemy, but now providing shelter for our C.O., Adjutant, Orderly Room staff, runners, signallers and officers' servants, all huddled together, with the shells bumping outside. One dark night when the mail and the rations arrived at this concrete cell, we noticed Col. Stewart open a parcel containing a cake and some cigarettes, and after he had ordered tea to be made for everybody, we saw him passing round the contents of that parcel, now in sixteen small but equal divisions. On the muddy floor sat the grandson of the ninth Earl of Galloway, in the middle of a dirty unshaven crowd, each man munching a chunk of cake and holding a handful of cigarettes. One can still see the Colonel sitting there, a charming smile on his kind, intellectual face.

On leaving the line we moved back to Ridge Wood, near Vierstraat. In happier days, even in winter, this must have been a delightful wood, but now in war-time it was an uninviting place, with big barren Nissen huts among the bare trees, and ditches for the unwary to stumble over at night—huts where on November mornings the water in our washing-bowls would become a sheet of ice in less than an hour. Nearby was a road-junction, called Confusion Corner. Many other thoroughfares in the neighbourhood of Ypres had even more suggestive names such as Hell-fire Corner, V.C. Road, Windy Corner and Salvation Corner.

* * *

In recalling those dark winter nights in Ridge Wood one remembers with horror the working parties which left each evening in the dusk to face toil and possibly death up there in the dreadful Spoil Bank defences. Four abreast they set out, in skeleton equipment, with arms and ammunition. Presently, after trudging along in dogged silence over a shell-pocked road, they form into single file and come to duckboards that tilt forward with a squelch as weary feet tread them down. "Make way there!" they hear, as files of men pass down the trench on their right. Then "Mind the wire!" as a fellow in front stumbles and rises with a suppliant oath. So on with broken step and heavy breathing, past the dim light coming up from a dug-out where a man is warming up something tasty and whistling "There's a long, long trail," until another fifty yards or so ahead the R.E. Corporal appears. Then, some struggling with baulks of timber or coils of barbed wire, others hoisting shovels and picks, the party moves on to its dangerous task. They reach the scene of the job, a Verey light goes up and everybody stands rigid and still in the ghostly glare, realizing that movement means a swift and horrible death. . . . The night drags on . . . stakes are driven noisily into the ground, and barbed wire is uncoiled with curses and mutterings. Only ten minutes to go, and time will be up . . . only five minutes . . . then a blinding crash and a frenzied shout "Stretcher-bearer! Stretcher-bearer!" . . .

The working party limps back to Ridge Wood, worn out with exhaustion and nerves, some having gone to the Casualty Clearing Station for the wounded, and some left behind lying dead in the wreckage and filth of the Salient.

CHAPTER IX

STILL IN THE SALIENT

NOVEMBER 1917, and still in the Salient.

After a period in Curragh Camp, not far from the village of Locre, we moved into the line which ran from Bitter Wood to North Farm, in the Klein Zillebeke area, another shell-hole system of trenches. The weather was now more severe than ever, snow alternating with frost, and, with deadly mustard-gas shells coming over at frequent intervals and the ground all torn up and hard as flint, our night patrols had a nerve-racking time.

It was now December 21st, and we were back in Ridge Wood thinking of Christmas and wondering how many more winters we should have to endure before we again saw the holly sticking out of a steaming plum pudding at home. Whenever anyone reminded us that *John Bull* had prophesied months ago that the War would be over by Christmas, his comrades would retort "Yes; but which Christmas?"—a remark typical of our cynical resignation in this, our third winter in the trenches. As one fellow put it, "This blinking show won't end until the 1914 men are greybeards and all the war-babies are wearing tin hats. After all, the first seven years are the worst!"

But somehow we kept our sense of humour. We even made a joke of that uninspired list of printed sentences—the official Field Post-Card, and extended its scope by various ingenious deletions of our own. One dull day every member of a certain Platoon amused himself by sending a Field Post-Card to his Sergeant, then on leave, and the forty or more greetings which came through the Sergeant's domestic letter-box in an avalanche bore nearly as many different messages, though the "hope to be discharged soon" was pretty general.

Leave! How we dreamed about it for months before the longed-for green ticket came our way! In 1915 it had been a mere nine days, two of them entirely spent in travelling; but it was gradually extended, until, towards the end of the War, the "Other Ranks" enjoyed a whole fortnight in England at intervals varying from nine to eighteen months. We began to look forward to our next spell from the very moment of leaving Victoria Station—that "Gate of Goodbye"—and this hope kept up our spirits in the blackest moments of mud and discomfort and despair. We even congratulated men with fairly slight wounds—"Blighty" wounds—which would ensure weeks, perhaps months at home. More and more we yearned for home and the end of all this horror.

But there was yet nearly a year to go. The celebration of Christmas 1917 was postponed till New Year's Day, when, back in Curragh Camp, the Corporals and Riflemen had a big feed in the cinema at Locre and other diversions to help them recapture the spirit of the season. On the following evening the Officers celebrated. So did the Warrant Officers and Sergeants, who, becoming thoroughly merry about midnight, decided to go and rag the Officers' Mess. On the morrow sundry black eyes and bruises, supplementing the universal "thick head," testified to the glorious scrimmages which had ensued; but it said much for the happy relations between officers and men of the Thirteenth that discipline remained unimpaired. Indeed, the bond of comradeship was strengthened by this seasonable lapse in official dignity.

When only a few days of January 1918 had gone by, we started a tour of the trenches in the region of Bulgar and Bitter Woods, our reconnoitring parties going out every night to explore the ground shortly to be covered by a raiding party of four officers and 70 other ranks, who had been undergoing special training for some time previously. The raid took place on the night of January 9th, and our fellows succeeded in storming a number of sentry-posts and dug-outs and inflicting severe casualties on the enemy,

STILL IN THE SALIENT

who was taken completely by surprise. It was a fine military success, but unfortunately we lost three wounded and three missing.

On January 12th, after one night in our old huts in Ridge Wood we took train to Eblingham, and marched from there to La Sablonière, a cheerful little village not far from Aire. Here we all began to renew some of our weakened vitality, and during the next three weeks we thoroughly enjoyed the peace of the countryside and all those distractions which Col. Stewart made it his first duty to provide whenever the Battalion was out of sound of the guns. Naturally, we still had our fair share of drill parades and spit and polish, too much, in fact, for some of the lads who were now being drafted to us. We recall one of these, a frail-looking youth who was brought to the Orderly Room and given three days Field Punishment for a trivial offence described thus on the charge sheet: "Not complying with an order, i.e. when told to double up failing to do so." He did not appear to have sufficient energy to run at the double at all. The physique of the old Battalion was now far below its original standard.

Like all periods of rest for the Infantry, our stay at La Sablonière quickly petered out, and we soon marched off again to join that brave garrison defending the ruins of the old city of

Ypres, once the pride of all Belgium. After spending a few days in hutments in Forrester and Scottish Woods, near Dickebusch, and another short period at Manawatu Camp—so named by the New Zealanders—we moved up to the Support line on the Menin Road, with Battalion Headquarters in the dug-outs of the Hooge Crater. This was a place frequently visited by enemy shells, and one sunny morning a 5·9 landed on the road above the Crater, sending a shower of hot metal flying downwards quite near a couple of war-bitten N.C.O.'s who happened to be seated at the time behind a screen of sacking. Then, in unseemly haste, not stopping to consider what a sight they presented to their pals—but no! their farcical reaction to the intrusion must be left to the imagination: it cannot be recorded in print.

On the night of March 6th we were in the front line facing the battered remnant of Polderhoek Château, when a young German, quite easily captured, and brought back to Glencorse Wood, caused a sensation in Battalion Headquarters by stating that his regiment was going to attack our trenches the following morning. As it was already midnight, the Adjutant, Orderly Room Staff, and runners were hard put to it to get orders into the hands of the Company Commanders in time; but when morning came,

STILL IN THE SALIENT 117

with everyone standing-to, and all eyes strained on the opposite trenches, nothing happened. It was simply a ruse of old Jerry's to let that youth wander into our lines with a false story. The raid actually took place two nights later, when we were acting as Reserve troops back at Manawatu Camp. As the K.R.R.'s who had taken our place in the trenches had been thrown out of them by the Germans, who were now in absolute possession, we had to go back again up the Menin Road to act as Support Battalion; but apart from carrying up huge supplies of bombs and S.A.A., we took no part in the counter-attack made the next morning. The 10th R.F. who launched that offensive included a large number of boys of eighteen, who were having their first experience in battle, and the Jerries received such a terrific hiding that not a single one of them got back to his trenches.

During the first three weeks of March, we shared with other units the duty of manning the front and Support lines in the Polderhoek sector, a tragic place where in that short period we lost 97 killed or wounded.

On the night of March 27th we returned for the last time from the trenches of the Ypres Salient. Back we came along the ghastly Menin Road, where, on either side, the wreckage of limbers, tanks, machine-guns and rifles was lying among great waterlogged holes which glistened every now and then under star shells hovering and flickering in the sky behind. Silently we plodded along—fags out—no talking; not a sound save the dull thud of marching feet, and the rustle of jolting equipment.

*   *   *

We spent the next day in huts in the neighbourhood of Nippenhoek, and then, very early the next morning, we boarded the train at the Hopoutre siding, near Poperinghe, taking a long last look at the barren wastes of Flanders, and thinking of comrades among the vast company sleeping up there in No Man's Land. We still remember them, those loyal pals, and we wonder if sometimes they hear the bugle sounded at dusk from the arched Menin Gate, sending out the sad, sweet notes of the Last Post across the ramparts of Ypres.

CHAPTER X

OLD HAUNTS AND NEW 1918

ON leaving the Ypres Salient we journeyed for thirty-six hours in horse-wagons, so familiar to all "Other Ranks" then using the French State Railways, and arrived at Bouquemaison on March 30, 1918. We then marched to Doullens, and from there had another train-ride to a suburb of Amiens, where we started a long night march to Pont Noyelles, finishing at 4 a.m. After a few hours' rest we boarded motor-lorries and were jolted as far as Marieux, a little place four miles from Doullens, where we had got on the train at six o'clock the previous evening! But we were not really surprised at all this circling about, since we knew that most of the movements of Infantry were planned more to deceive spies than to secure the physical and mental happiness of the troops. At Marieux we were temporarily housed in an old aerodrome, rather a suitable place we thought for a Battalion so often taking to wings.

On the night of April 1st we went into the trenches in the Gommecourt sector, and occupied a position very near the line which we had garrisoned nearly three years before—the line which looked out on the lone poplar standing in the Hannescamps Ravine. All of the original Battalion who still survived seemed glad to be back in the old haunts of 1915, and no doubt many were wondering if the young rats in the trenches were now grandfathers, if Madame in the little estaminet near the Bienvillers duck-pond was still serving *vin blanc* and *vin rouge*, and if the apple-trees in the orchards of Fon-quevillers were again beginning to blossom.

*   *   *

On April 8th, at dusk, a great tragedy befell the 13th Rifle Brigade—the death of our beloved C.O., Lieut.-Col. W. R. Stewart, D.S.O., M.C., killed by a sniper. It was a terrible blow, for we all regarded him as an ideal Battalion Commander—a brilliant soldier, a kind, considerate man who never forgot the welfare of his troops, who overlooked their failings, who dispensed justice with a human touch, and who gave a forgiving smile instead of a rebuke. He was only thirty when he died. He was buried with full military honours at Couin, a tiny place on a hill behind the line, and one can still see the sad funeral procession moving slowly up the village street, led by the Divisional Band playing Chopin's Funeral March, and the flag-draped coffin followed by a small company of N.C.O. bearers who were mourning the loss of a friend.

No Commanding Officer better deserved the garland of remembrance and affection which we offered him on that spring afternoon as the silver bugles sounded the Last Post and the Firing Party sent their volleys over his grave.

* * *

Lieut.-Col. H. S. C. Richardson took over the command of the Battalion on April 12th, and that night we moved into the Support trenches; but we were not there long, for we soon relieved the 13th Battalion of the A.I.F. in the front line in Hebuterne. Those Aussies were first-rate fighting men, and before handing over they told us how, with nearly a hundred snipers pushed out in front, they had worried the Jerries who were all cramped up in a half-dug trench, and how many bull's-eyes they had made on a grey target since their arrival in that sector. "Nothing like it since Gallipoli," they declared. But the "diggers" soon left our Division, because, so it was said, their ideas of discipline were all wrong, especially their unpardonable failure to acknowledge the difference between a common soldier and an English officer of exalted rank.

It had certainly been an education to our fellows at Ridge Wood six months earlier to see a party of Australians lined up on parade, some in slouch helmets, some in cap comforters, some in tin hats. The 2nd Lieutenant in charge of us gasped at the way they numbered off in a lazy sing-song; but he went stiff with horror when one "digger" not only produced a battered cigarette, but strolled out of the ranks to his officer, remarking, "Say, Bill! Give us a light!"

After a short stay in bivouacs at Coigneux, where the German night-bombers and long-range guns gave us little peace, we marched to Louvencourt, when Col. Richardson left us to join the 2nd Rifle Brigade. It was here, at Louvencourt, just before the arrival of Lieut.-Col. R. A. Mostyn-Owen, our new C.O., that a note came from Division in continuation of a previous communication from the same source, urging Commanding Officers to cut down the men's rations. The note contained the following illuminating paragraphs:

> The quantity of rations underdrawn in many units continues to be almost negligible, whereas in certain others of the same branch of the Service, of equal strength and exactly similarly situated, the underdrawals are encouraging. That the present high scale of rations is not really needed by the men will be made evident to anyone who will visit the baths and see the men stripped, and notice the remarkable condition of fatness of most men, which certainly cannot conduce to great exertions or fitness for hard fighting or marching.
>
> It must be remembered, too, that the canteens and estaminets retail an enormous quantity of foodstuffs.

It is considered that at least 25 per cent. rations can be underdrawn without ill results to anyone.

Major J. B. G. Taylor, M.C., was temporarily in command of the Battalion at the time, and fortunately for us, he had a sense of humour, combined with an appreciation of the truth regarding the rations drawn by the 13th Rifle Brigade; happily, too, he had no desire to see his men wallowing in obesity and dirty bath water. So he took no action, but no doubt he thought some hard things about the author of this perfect example of the pestiferous piffle turned out by a certain type of Staff Officer who resided in a comfortable château well behind the line.

One often got disgusted at the stupid inability of such people to appreciate the realities of the trenches, best illustrated, perhaps, in the message delivered to our Orderly Room Sergeant in the line, whilst the tragic attack on the German trenches on July 10, 1916, was actually in progress. It ran:

> Report immediately number of Verey pistols on charge AAA. 1 in. and 1½ in. separately.

* * *

From Louvencourt we travelled in motor-lorries to Souastre, another village which brought back memories of 1915, and on the same night, April 24th, we went into the front line opposite Ablainzeville. For some time afterwards we were in that sector, either in the front line or in the Support trenches, all the time sustaining heavy losses in killed and wounded.

On May 8th a daylight attack on a large scale was launched at Bucquoy, with the object of advancing the outpost line so as to obtain better observation of the valley in which the enemy was entrenched.

Two companies were detailed for the assault, and they went Over the Top at 2 p.m. The Right Company soon gained their objective (Doll's House) and remained in possession for some time, until they were practically surrounded by a large force of the enemy, who compelled them to retire, by which time they had lost 60 per cent. of their number. Meanwhile another of our storming parties was pushing on, but they, too, had to withdraw owing to heavy enfilade fire from machine-guns. Elsewhere the operation was proceeding successfully, and after an enemy machine-gun had been captured and the crew put out of action, our main force encountered a large muster of Germans, who were wiped out entirely except for eleven prisoners. At this stage our fellows were in a cemetery, and with 2nd Lieut. G. D. Frazer wounded, Sergt. Gregg took charge and led his men in a furious struggle with the Jerries, who were making full use of the cover offered by the tombstones and vaults of the civilian dead, until the far side of the cemetery was reached. Then the Germans made a determined counter-attack, working round our flanks and gradually pressing our men back; but Sergt. Gregg was a fellow who scorned defeat, so, with his party reinforced after suffering heavy casualties, he pushed forward with his men and pulverized the opposition after some terrific hand-to-hand fighting. While all this was happening, our remaining raiders were smashing their way through, all helping most gallantly to ensure the success of that daring venture carried out in broad daylight.

The outstanding heroes of the day were Sergt. Gregg and Rfn. Beesley,* who were awarded Victoria Crosses for their conspicuous bravery and initiative. A full account of their heroic deeds is given in Appendix III.

The offensive operation was carried out at great cost to the Battalion, a large number having been killed, including 2nd Lieut. J. Forrester. The death-roll was increased to 49 a month later when 2nd Lieut. G. D. Frazer died of his wounds.

* * *

* Rfn. Beesley was promoted to Corporal later.

After periods in barns at Souastre, in the trenches in the village of Essarts, in a camp at Authie and in the Reserve line between Sailly-au-Bois and Hebuterne, we went into huts at Bois-du-Warnimont. From there on the night of June 5th we went off in motor-lorries to Bouvelles, reached at nine o'clock the next morning, and then, later the same day, we marched to Guinemicourt, where we remained in Corps Reserve for three days. We then marched to Sains-en-Amienois, a pleasant village just behind the firing-line, and acted as support troops to the French.

The *poilus* were most friendly, and let us use their well-stocked canteen, where champagne could be bought for a remarkably low sum; but we rather disgusted a few of them when an enemy airman came over one evening and brought down an empty French observation balloon. They simply couldn't understand that in cheering that German flier as the balloon came down in flames, we were only showing how we admired a fellow who had the pluck to pass three times through a heavy barrage of "Archies." We had another illustration of the different mentality of our Allies during the War years when we saw a group of their soldiers listening to a show given by our Divisional Concert Party, and arguing heatedly among themselves whether a female impersonator was a man or a woman. True, the performer was well made up and in his nicely cut gown obtained from his wife, a Red-Cross nurse in Paris, he looked really attractive; but even so, the French really did us a great injustice in thinking that we carted a woman round with us.

As we were not called into action after all, we gradually withdrew from this front, stopping for a time at a village farther back named Nampty, where we enjoyed an afternoon of water sports in a river. Leaving Loeuilly on the night of June 21st, we journeyed by train to Mondicourt, arriving there at two o'clock the following morning, and then marching to Henu, two places well remembered by the few who had managed to survive the past three years. It was from Mondicourt station that the leave train used to start in the winter of 1915.

* * *

It was somewhere about this time that an appeal was made to the men to reduce the length of their letters home, so as to make it less of a burden to the censoring officers. The older Riflemen were just then so fed up with the War that, on principle, they refrained from referring to it more than they could help; but many of the younger lads in writing to their people innocently disclosed bits of military information, sometimes adding a pinhole or two which, with the sheet fitted over a duplicate map kept at home, and the two punctured together, would reveal in what part of France the writer was at the time.

This official request for shorter letters made one N.C.O. curious as to the reason. So he consulted his officer, who informed him quite seriously that a man had recently sent a letter to be censored which was seven feet long!... "But, sir," exclaimed the Sergeant, "How on earth ...?" It transpired that the correspondent was an officer's servant who had purloined a length of his master's toilet-roll. Seven feet of correspondence was rather too much of a good thing, but for once the perforations were allowed to pass.

* * *

We were back again in the Bucquoy sector, and from now until the end of the first fortnight in August we spent our days doing tours of the front line, followed by periods in the Support trenches at Essarts, in the Reserve line in Pigeon Wood, and finally in the barns of Souastre. It was during one of our spells at Souastre that a big German bomber came over one night in the moonlight, and, apparently taking our travelling kitchens for a battery of guns, dropped an aerial torpedo right in the middle of a crowd of sleeping cooks, killing all of them and making a hole, which, when measured the next day, turned out to be twenty feet deep and forty-two feet in diameter. One of the victims was poor Freddy Ellis, a veteran of the Soudan and Boer campaigns, who had joined up again in 1914.

* * *

The Battalion was in the front-line trenches facing Ablainzeville on the night of August 20th, waiting for the signal that would set the whole front ablaze with the great attack that had been planned for the entire British Army. On this summer night, with an ominous silence brooding over our line, men were contemplating what the morrow's ordeal would bring to them. Would they come through unscathed? Would it be a "blighty one," and a nice period in hospital—not too painful, but long enough to keep one in England until the end of the War, which surely could not be far off now? Would it be a slow, lingering death, with horrible suffering? Or a swift end—just a passing out like the flight of that swallow which had been twittering overhead all day? . . .

Still, why worry? Sleep would come all right to-night with an extra ration of rum. . . .

CHAPTER XI

THE BIG SHOW

A THICK mist hung over our line at zero hour on the morning of August 21, 1918, forming a useful screen for our advance which started at 4.30 a.m., and had for its objective the German trenches on the outskirts of Ablainzeville. Our fellows carried everything before them as they swept on to the enemy's position and captured it, happily with not a great number of casualties.

At zero hour plus fifty minutes, the 63rd (R.N.) Division—old companions of ours in the Battles of the Ancre and Arras—passed over the scene of our success and proceeded to attack the enemy lines in Logeast Wood, intending then to go on to Achiet-le-Grand. They captured the wood, but, so tough was the opposition, they could get no farther. On the night of August 22nd, therefore, we were warned to carry out this unfulfilled task, and on the following morning, under cover of a creeping barrage, the men of the 13th Rifle Brigade went forward to assault the German trenches to the West of Achiet, a position with strong natural defences and one of great strategical importance to the enemy. Some very fierce fighting now

Imperial War Museum photograph] [*Copyright reserved*
H.M. THE KING PRESENTING THE V.C. TO CORPORAL BEESLEY.

Imperial War Museum photograph] [*Copyright reserved*
CORPL. BEESLEY AND SERGT. GREGG ADMIRING THEIR V.C.'s

took place, especially on a railway embankment lined with large numbers of machine-guns and trench mortars, but the speed and thoroughness of our attack, ably directed by Col. Mostyn-Owen, was too much for the opposition, obstinate though it was. Shortly after noon the Battalion was holding a strongly fortified position about 1,000 yards East of the railway embankment, and within an hour not only Achiet, but Bihucourt as well, was in our possession. During that day's fighting the Thirteenth took over 500 prisoners, 40 heavy machine-guns, 70 light machine-guns, 20 trench mortars, 10 tank guns, one 4·2 cm. gun and one 77 mm. gun.

In accordance with orders received during the previous night the Battalion advanced on the morning of August 24th with the object of straightening out the existing salient by capturing the high ground North of Biefvillers, an operation completely successful. Next day we had orders to exploit our gains, so strong patrols were sent out and by 2 p.m. these parties were holding some ground West of Favreuil, with the New Zealanders quickly advancing on the right. Later in the afternoon we were told to attack Favreuil, and at 6 p.m. we were assembled at a point some 800 yards short of that place, by which time the enemy was heavily bombarding the valley which led up to the village. Half an hour later our fellows went forward, just as the Germans were coming out in great numbers to launch a counter-attack. The two forces met midway to the village, and some heavy fighting at close quarters followed, but in the end the Germans gave up the struggle, leaving us in possession of Favreuil and over 400 prisoners. Soon afterwards the K.R.R.C., who were on our left and experiencing considerable trouble from machine-guns, sent out an appeal for help, so the Royal Fusiliers went forward to deal with the situation. In the meantime, men of the Rifle Brigade were advancing to their new objective, some German trenches about 150 yards farther on, and after some stiff fighting they captured it with a lot more prisoners and machine-guns. When darkness came it was found that there were nests of enemy snipers and machine-gunners still in the village; but eventually all these troublesome fellows were either killed or captured, and by eleven o'clock that night we had established a strong defence line.

The operations carried out from August 21st to 25th had been extraordinarily successful, for we had captured more territory in that short period than during the whole of the past three years. The prisoners taken numbered well over 1,000 with enough guns and material of all sorts to fill a large field; yet the enemy put up a fine defence and bravely disputed every yard of ground, his counter-attacks being particularly fierce and skilfully planned. The 13th R.B. had distinguished itself once again—but at a price. We lost 14 officers and 406 other ranks, nearly half the strength of the Battalion as it was on the morning of August 21st, and the long death-roll included Capt. F. W. Lindley-Gull, 2nd Lieuts. J. K. Ferrier, G. B. Spencer and R. Turnbull, M.C., and scores of equally gallant N.C.O.'s and men, many of them old comrades since 1914.

On coming out of action on the morning of August 26th, we went back to Logeast Wood, where we had rested after capturing Ablainzeville.

We moved later to huts not far from Favreuil, and then up to a position West of Havrincourt, where we saw a big German nightbomber brought down with his crew of eight. He was coming over to lay his eggs, when the brilliant beam of a searchlight caught him, and before he could get back into the darkness he was met by one of our planes, returning from a reconnaisance over the enemy lines. One short burst from the British airman's machine-gun, a frantic attempt by the Gotha to straighten out, and then a nose-dive in flames at terrific speed, a crash, and the simultaneous explosion of the cargo of bombs. The pilot-officer, however, escaped in a parachute though he was nearly killed by a group of Artillerymen who had suffered badly from night bombing.

During the late afternoon of September 11th the Battalion moved forward to a point of assembly, ready for an attack to be made the next morning, in the course of which 2nd Lieut. F. T. Rice was killed. This young officer had formerly been an N.C.O. in the Battalion, going home from France to a cadet school at the same time as Sergt. A. H. Halford (who got the D.C.M. with us in 1916, and was killed in 1918 when a Captain in the 2nd R.B.). Poor Rice had had a strong premonition of death on the day before he was killed, as, indeed, had many others, including Rfn. Honour, a Headquarters runner killed on the Ancre, and Capt. Bowyer who died in the Battle of Arras.

At 5.25 on the morning of September 12th, the Battalion was ready for the attack on Trescault Spur, with "B" and "D" Companies in the front line, "C" Company in support, and "A" Company in reserve. After being delayed for a time by heavy machine-gun fire, the assault was launched, and when all the enemy's strong points had been seized, the two leading Companies stormed and captured their objective. An hour later, with assistance from a T.M. Battery, the advance was continued, till at last, after heavy fighting, the Battalion was in possession of the whole of the enemy's trenches, whilst large crowds of German prisoners were streaming back to the cages in the rear. That evening "D" Company's new position was heavily bombarded and then attacked by a strong force of the enemy. Small parties of Germans managed to re-establish themselves in this position, but they were soon turned out again, leaving behind a large number of dead and wounded, together with six machine-guns, a trench mortar, much ammunition and a complete telephone outfit.

At six o'clock the next morning "D" Company was withdrawn to the Reserve line, having sustained heavy losses during the previous day's fighting. The only survivors above the rank of Lance-Corporal were Capt. P. F. Davy, M.C., and Corpl. Faggeter. The day passed without any important incident until, soon after 6 p.m., the enemy launched a counter-attack against our Right Company, but he was driven off. About the same time our Left Company were also dealing with a similar offensive, but much stronger and fiercer, during which about 15 Germans got a temporary footing in the trench, only to be overpowered. The few poor devils who started to run back to their line got no farther than some barbed wire in which they became entangled.

By 8.50 that night our newly won position

was firmly established, but, as the enemy sent over gas shells all night long, there was not much peace for us. The next afternoon we had to send out two platoons to guard one of our flanks, but the threatened attack by the Germans did not take place, so we moved out of the trenches that night to a position West of Havrincourt Wood and near Velu. Next day we went still farther back, to Lebecquière, and remained there until we again marched forward to Havrincourt Wood, at very short notice. However, the expected counter-attack did not come, so we returned to Lebecquière. Four moves in four days were sufficiently exhausting; but it was no use grousing, and we accepted every experience as it came, realizing that we were just pieces on a chessboard which changed more and more rapidly as the end of the Game approached.

On September 20th we went right away from the trenches, first to Ligny-Thilloy, then to a place called Pys. And "peace" we found there for a while, long hours of rest in huts and bivouacs, some of us in dug-outs immediately below the graves in the civilian cemetery.

We planned to hold Battalion Sports, but before the proposed date we were suddenly marched away to Villers-au-Flos, and then on to a position North-East of Gonnelieu.

Our casualties that September had been eight officers and 235 other ranks. Among the dead were 2nd Lieut. C. E. Hadwen, Sergt. C. W. Sanders, D.C.M., Sergt. T. Woof, M.M., and a large number of other good pals. The Reaper had been busy again.

CHAPTER XII

LAST SCENE OF ALL

ON October 1, 1918, we relieved the 2nd Canterbury Battalion of the New Zealand Force in the front line, West of the Canal at Vaucelles. Here we stayed for a few days, and the patrols sent out at night to reconnoitre the position on the other side of the Canal had some thrilling experiences. A party in charge of Sergt. Shoesmith—who, happily, was spared to return to his job as golf professional—had a most exciting time when they were in a house one dark night and heard gutteral speech outside.

The Germans were now gradually falling back, so when we heard on the morning of October 5th that their advance posts in front of us had been vacated, we started off in pursuit of the retreating enemy until we reached a position West of Belle Aise Farm, a position which we quickly fortified against possible attack.

When tanks came up a few nights later, the Battalion supplied escorts for these monsters, and also despatched a whole Company to give support to the 10th R.F., who were due to attack on the following morning. On completion of our duties, we went forward to Guillemin Farm, and then on to Ligny-en-Cambresis, where we spent several days. The villagers we saw were nearly all old folk, haggard and drawn, the retreating Germans having taken the younger men and women back to work for them. The enemy had laid all sorts of traps for the advancing British, such as bombs hidden in pianos and fireplaces, but we were too wary to be caught. The church tower of Ligny was mined, but the engineers soon saw to that.

We moved to Bethincourt on October 21st, and from there to Briastre, where the body of dear old Hardy, the V.C. Chaplain, was lying awaiting burial. Not far away was the place where men of the Rifle Brigade—"Old Contemptibles"—had first met the enemy in action in the autumn of 1914.

Early on the morning of October 23rd we marched forward to a position behind troops of the Fifth Division, who were due to initiate a big advance that day. Owing to the temporary failure of the attack we had to stand-by for a time, but at 10 a.m. we went forward, protected by a creeping barrage, and after a fierce fight secured our objective. Scores of prisoners were taken, among them a Company Commander, accompanied by a little batman carrying his master's valise. This servant seemed delighted to be captured, and told some of our boys at Headquarters that when our bombardment started that morning he had advised his chum to " 'op it and give himself up." He asked us in rich Cockney how things were looking in dear old Piccadilly, and explained that before the War he had been employed by a London hairdresser.

Later the same morning the Battalion carried on the advance, and that night went into billets in the village of Beaurain.

The end of October found us at Neuville, where we had been since leaving Beaurain a week before. Our losses during the month were rather fewer than in August and September, but still very heavy—8 officers and 107 other ranks.

On the night of November 3rd the 13th R.B. moved up to an assembly position and prepared for its last battle in the Great War.

* * *

At five o'clock the next morning, November 4th, "A," "C" and "D" Companies were waiting in the Black Line, with "B" Company in reserve in the cellars of Ghissignies, and at 5.34 the signal was given. "D" Company were on the right of the attacking force, closely supported by two Platoons of "A" Company, and they moved forward towards a railway embankment, where the enemy was holding a strongly fortified position. Our fellows were now fighting like men possessed, and nothing could stop them. On and on they pressed, continuing the ferocious struggle, in which no quarter was given on either side until the enemy's resistance was completely smashed. Fifty prisoners and 12 machine-guns were captured in that encounter.

The attack was now irresistible, and the advancing troops were soon pushing on towards the Blue Line, where all the German strong points were mopped up in spite of considerable trouble from trench mortars and machine-guns.

While "D" Company were fighting their way to success, the men of "C" Company were pushing ahead; but they, too, met with stiff opposition and their right flank was temporarily checked. The left flank, however, assisted by a Platoon of "A" Company, carried all before it and succeeded in going up with "D" Company to the Blue Line, taking 40 prisoners as well as a number of trench mortars and machine-guns.

"B" Company left Ghissignies at 6 a.m. Noticing that the advance of his men was being checked by machine-gun fire, the Company Commander organized an assault by two Platoons in co-operation with a tank and trench mortars. This move led to tremendous fighting at close quarters, but the enemy's resistance was eventually overcome and 70 prisoners taken, along with a number of machine-guns. "B" Company and the remainder of "C" and "A" Companies then advanced to the Blue Line.

But the task of the Battalion had been only partially completed, so at 8 a.m. the attack was continued towards the Blue Dotted Line. The advancing forces were now under heavy shellfire, but they pressed on, engaging the Germans in a deadly struggle and compelling them to surrender in large numbers. Isolated enemy posts still gave trouble, but in the end they were all wiped out.

Nothing could stop the men of the Thirteenth, and they reached their final objective within fifty minutes, the whole position being firmly consolidated by 10.30 a.m. Although greatly reduced in numbers, the Battalion continued to hold this position until eight o'clock that night, when the relieving force came into the line.

Signal communication had been most difficult during the battle owing to the heavy shellfire, while visual communication was ruled out by a heavy mist, yet the signallers worked heroically all the time trying to mend broken lines in a storm of shells and machine-gun bullets. The runners, on whom an extra burden fell, also behaved gallantly, and a large number of them were killed or wounded in trying to get through with written messages.

LT.-COL. R. A. MOSTYN-OWEN, D.S.O.
Commanding the Battalion from April 1918 until its disbandment.

By brilliant leadership, splendid initiative and heroic endeavour, the 13th R.B. achieved great distinction on the battlefield that November day; everyone, from the Colonel down to the last recruited Rifleman, did his part nobly and well. It was a fitting end to the Battalion's long and glorious record as a fighting unit.

What of the cost? Again a tragic story—157 killed, wounded or missing. In the long list of the dead were the names of many who had been with us a long time, including Capt. P. F. Davy, M.C., Lieuts. G. S. Hunter and J. Macaulay, and a vast company of splendid fellows serving in the ranks.

*　　　　*　　　　*

During that final offensive, whilst the battle was raging furiously, men of the Thirteenth heard the drone of a British aeroplane above the racket of the machine-guns and the crashing of shells and bombs; flying low, it met a withering burst of enemy machine-gun fire, and presently some of us, looking up, saw the solitary airman fall forward over his cockpit and thence to the ground. When we picked him up, a slender figure in flying kit, we found he was a young officer of our own whom we all loved, Capt. R. Colvill-Jones, M.C., who had come to us after the Somme, and went away in May 1918 to join the R.A.F. He had left his home in Buenos Aires in 1914 to serve, first of all as a plain Rifleman, and his kindly smile had brightened many dark moments during the years when he was an officer with the Thirteenth. Did he recognize the troops engaging the enemy beneath the sweep of his wings that misty winter morning? It is a question which remains unanswered, but it is beyond all shadow of doubt that, had he known of his impending fate, he could have had no greater wish than to be buried, as he was, by his old comrades of the Rifle Brigade.

CHAPTER XIII

THE CURTAIN RINGS DOWN

COMING out of the Battle Area on the morning of November 5, 1918, we moved back to Beaurain, and remained there six days. Rumours were now going round the Battalion that the end of the War was in sight; but many of us were still incredulous though the Brigadier had said that the Ghissignies attack would be our last. It all seemed too good to be true—this talk of Peace —especially as prisoners were still pouring into the cages near at hand, some of them still defiant, and German night-bombers yet raided the neighbourhood of our billets.

But at last, on the morning of November 11th, we heard a military policeman shout, "It's all over, boys!" as he directed the traffic on our march still farther West. Not even then were some of us convinced.

"Hear that?" said somebody; "the blinking War's over!"

"Is it?" grunted someone else. "Then ask him who's won!"

But when we reached Caudry and heard the official announcement that an Armistice had been signed that morning in a wood on the French front, down South, we knew that it was true.

But still we went about dazed, men in a dream.

Gradually we realized that at last the Curtain had rung down, and that all those still on the Stage would never again face the mud and blood of the trenches. No more standing in those filthy ditches in the Ypres Salient, no more ghastly working parties, no more waiting for zero hour, no more of that sickening ache which preceded the journey Over the Top, no more of the blinding storm of shell-fire and the awful racket of machine-guns, no more bloody hand-to-hand fighting, no more the fear of impending death....

It was as if a night-cloud had lifted at the approach of morning.

*   *   *

That night the Battalion tried to forget. First of all we trooped down to the Grande Place, where John Dennis and his boys played rollicking tunes in the dim light of candles held by some of us over well-thumbed music. Everybody was there. The Padre was all smiles. Even the pathetic townspeople did their best to look happy as we shouted the old familiar songs and tried to dance in our great cigar-box boots. Fun was already beginning in billets and in the Officers' and Sergeants' Messes. Far into the night the noise of celebration continued, and nobody wanted to rouse next morning when the Sergeants came round shouting, "Come on there! Show a leg!" Then, rubbing our eyes, we remembered—THE WAR WAS OVER!

Caudry was already astir. People were talking excitedly, smiling, even laughing—they who had almost forgotten how to laugh. The four years' torture was really over. Never again would German officers push them off the pavements. Never again! Down came all the threatening notices, all the *Verbotens* and the *Achtungs*. Out came the treasured bottles of wine, so carefully hidden in anticipation of this event and of the victorious Allied Army which would one day clatter up the cobbled streets.

On December 1st the Battalion said Goodbye to those hospitable people, and set out on its long trek into Belgium. Spending a night at Capelle, we marched to Preux-au-Sart, and after a twelve days' stay pushed on through Houdin, Louvroil, Erquellines, Merbies St. Marie and Fontaine l'Eveque, to Jumet, which we reached on December 20th. This Belgian town in the province of Hainaut, not far from Charleroi, was our final destination, and it said a lot for our fitness and discipline that not a single man had fallen out during the long march from Caudry, although the average distance was from ten to fourteen miles a day.

We spent more than four months at Jumet. Various garrison duties were carried out, and we had the inescapable drill and "poshing up"; but the play spirit was encouraged in every way, and there were lots of things like concerts and sports to keep us amused. At the Brigade Sports held in January we maintained our fine record as athletes by winning the cross-country run by more than 1,000 points. Then in February we had a Divisional Race Meeting, organized by our C.O., and the event was a great success.

Demobilization was now proceeding rapidly, and the number remaining to enjoy the delights of peace-time soldiering was getting less every month. On May 5, 1919, the last *cadre*, accompanied by Lieut.-Col. R. A. Mostyn-Owen, D.S.O., embarked for England.

*   *   *

The grand old Battalion was no more. Its work done, its glory ended, it faded out quietly, like the last whispering notes of a cathedral organ. Those of us still left often think of it with wistfulness, proudly recalling the illustrious record not dimmed by the passage of time.

A wise Providence has ordained that we should not remember too clearly, nor too often, the anguish of body and mind endured during those long years in the trenches of France and Flanders. But what we never forget, nor ever shall till the end of our lives, are the great moments we shared, the comradeship born of mutual hardship and suffering, the wonderful understanding of each other, the unfailing loyalty, the sacred fellowship between man and man—all filling the Temple of Memory with an everlasting fragrance.

APPENDIX I

The Battalion's Losses in France and Belgium during the years 1915–1918.

	Killed or Died of Wounds		Sent Home Wounded or Sick (excluding Officers)
	Officers	Other Ranks	
1915	—	16	52
1916	10	173	632
1917	10	250	692
1918	17	292	772
	37	731	2,148

$$\underbrace{37 \qquad 731}_{768}$$

To the Roll of the Dead must be added all those who have died since the Armistice, many of them after a long and brave struggle with pain and weakness.

APPENDIX II

The Awards gained by Officers and other Ranks for Gallantry and good work in the Field while serving in the Battalion.*

THE VICTORIA CROSS †
Sergt. W. Gregg, D.C.M., M.M.
Rfn. W. Beesley.

THE DISTINGUISHED SERVICE ORDER
Lt.-Col. C. F. Pretor-Pinney.   Major A. N. Strode Jackson
Lt.-Col. W. R. Stewart, M.C.   (Bar).
Lt.-Col. R. A. Mostyn-Owen.   Major O. B. Graham.

THE MILITARY CROSS
2nd Lt. E. N. Ackroyd.   2nd Lt. J. Forrester.
2nd Lt. K. Archbold.   Capt. C. M. Gilray.
2nd Lt. J. McW. Bampfield.   2nd Lt. A. C. W. George.
Lieut. R. N. R. Blaker.   Lieut. H. W. Gosney.
2nd Lt. D. F. Bruce.   Lieut. G. S. Hunter.
2nd Lt. W. J. Carlile, M.M.   Capt. G. G. H. Irving.
2nd Lt. L. S. Chamberlen.   Lieut. W. T. Kerruish.
2nd Lt. G. W. H. Chambers.   Capt. L. G. N. Langmead.
2nd Lt. R. Colvill-Jones.   2nd Lt. A. A. B. McDonald.
2nd Lt. A. L. Cooper (Bar).   Lieut. E. C. Martin.
Capt. P. F. Davy.   2nd Lt. J. C. H. Mathams
2nd Lt. T. H. Fielding.   (Bar).
2nd Lt. G. E. G. Fitzgibbon.   Capt. W. W. Nothard (Bar).

* Many of the awards included in this list were posthumous awards, while many others were received by Officers and Men who at a later date either were killed in action or died of wounds.

In each instance the rank stated was that held at the time of the award.

† See also Appendix III.

Lieut. E. R. Pidsley.
Capt. A. W. Raymond, R.A.M.C. (Bar).
2nd Lt. J. C. Reepmaker.
2nd Lt. F. Simpson.
2nd Lt. G. C. Siordet.
2nd Lt. W. M. Smith.
Lieut. J. B. G. Taylor.
2nd Lt. J. F. Thoburn.
2nd Lt. W. Wallace.
2nd Lt. E. Walpole.
Capt. E. R. Wedemeyer.
2nd Lt. A. M. Wiseman.
Capt. E. W. Wood.
C.S.M. J. Croutcher.
C.S.M. F. J. Oliver, M.M.
C.S.M. C. H. Stenning, M.M.

THE DISTINGUISHED CONDUCT MEDAL

Cpl. F. Anthony.
Sergt. H. Bailey.
Sergt. W. A. Balchin.
Rfn. R. Barton.
C.S.M. G. Bishop.
C.S.M. T. Crane, M.M.
Cpl. H. Draper (Bar).
Sergt. W. Driscoll.
L/Cpl. W. P. Egles.
Sergt. M. Ellington.
Sergt. W. Gregg, M.M.
Sergt. A. H. Halford.
L/Cpl. R. H. Lewis.
Rfn. F. C. Luther.
Sergt. E. Manktelow, M.M.
C.S.M. W. D. Martin.
Sergt. J. A. Mitchell.
Sergt. A. E. Montgomery.
L/Cpl. J. E. Phillips.
Sergt. E. Phillips.
Sergt. C. W. Sanders.
Sergt. J. W. Stott, M.M.
Sergt. E. G. Thompson.
L/Cpl. E. Tyler.
Sergt. C. Wilson.
Cpl. H. Wisdom.

BAR TO THE DISTINGUISHED CONDUCT MEDAL

Sergt. N. Champion, D.C.M., M.M.*

* This N.C.O. won his D.C.M. while serving with another unit.

APPENDIX II

THE MILITARY MEDAL

Rfn. E. J. Adams.
L/Corpl. H. W. Allan.
Rfn. G. E. Allen.
Rfn. L. Appleton.
Rfn. A. J. Arnold.
Corpl. J. Bacon.
Rfn. W. B. Balkwill.
Corpl. F. Barlow.
L/Corpl. T. Beard.
Rfn. T. J. Beer.
Corpl. F. Blackmore.
Corpl. A. Bourne (Bar).
Rfn. F. Bradley.
L/Corpl. F. Brooker.
Rfn. A. A. Brown.
Sergt. C. Browne.
Rfn. T. Callery.
Corpl. H. Carpenter.
L/Sergt. N. Champion, D.C.M.
Sergt. A. Chilcott.
Rfn. J. Clark.
Corpl. J. R. Clarke.
Corpl. P. J. Clarke.
Sergt. G. W. G. Colclough.
Rfn. E. Coldwell.
Rfn. W. H. Collard.
Corpl. T. H. Collins.
L/Corpl. W. J. Cousins.
Rfn. P. A. Couzens.
Rfn. E. Cramp.
Sergt. T. Crane, D.C.M.
L/Corpl. G. V. Craston.
L/Sergt. G. Crook.
C.Q.M.S. B. Croxford.
Sergt. J. Curtis.
Rfn. W. Curtis.
L/Sergt. H. Davey.
Rfn. W. D. Davies.
Sergt. W. Davis.
Sergt. P. A. Denham.
Sergt. J. Dennis.
Rfn. J. T. Dillon.
Rfn. P. Douglas.
Corpl. G. Dunkling.
Rfn. A. Eaglestone.
Rfn. C. Eastment.
Rfn. E. Elleray.
Rfn. F. J. Ely (Bar).
L/Sergt. C. C. Evans.
Corpl. R. D. Farnfield.
Corpl. J. Finnigan.
C.Q.M.S. L. C. Fitch.
L/Corpl. T. Forth.
Corpl. J. W. Fowler.
Rfn. J. Fowler.
Corpl. W. Fowley.
Rfn. A. Frankish.
L/Sergt. A. Gardner.
Corpl. R. J. Gardner.
L/Sergt. H. S. Gaze.
Corpl. J. Gilbert.
Rfn. L. Gladman.
Rfn. F. H. Goodger.
L/Corpl. W. H. Goodman.
Sergt. P. Goodwin.

L/Corpl. W. Gregg.
L/Corpl. J. E. Grogan.
L/Corpl. J. Hancock.
Sergt. I. H. Hansell.
Sergt. A. H. Harris.
Rfn. J. Hardiker.
L/Corpl. L. Hartley.
L/Corpl. W. G. Hayward.
Rfn. F. Hedges.
Rfn. W. H. Hemsley.
L/Corpl. A. Hewit.
L/Sergt. O. D. Higgins.
Corpl. W. A. Hills.
L/Corp. J. C. Horam.
L/Corpl. J. Horsman.
L/Sergt. W. Hoyles.
L/Corpl. A. Hughes.
Rfn. H. F. J. Hunt.
L/Corpl. J. Hunt.
L/Corpl. H. Jackson.
Rfn. J. G. Jackson.
C.S.M. D. G. James.
Corpl. C. A. Johnson.
Sergt. N. Johnson.
Rfn. A. Kirby.
Rfn. F. Kirk.
Rfn. J. T. Last.
Rfn. M. D. Lear.
Corpl. A. Lee
Rfn. R. Lee.
Rfn. J. Leeke.
Corpl. J. H. Lees.
L/Corpl. W. Letchford.
Corpl. A. J. Liversedge.
Corpl. A. Lockyer.

L/Corpl. A. D. Louden.
Rfn. J. Mackey.
C.S.M. E. Manktelow, D.C.M.
Corpl. J. A. Manning.
Corpl. C. Martin.
Corpl. J. Maughan.
Rfn. A. E. Messenger.
Rfn. W. H. F. Minter.
Corpl. W. H. A. Monckton.
Rfn. A. Nash.
L/Corpl. J. A. Nicholls.
Rfn. J. Norris.
Rfn. F. G. Nurse.
Corpl. M. J. O'Connor (Bar).
C.S.M. F. J. Oliver, M.C.
Sergt. J. C. Orger.
Corpl. G. Otley.
Sergt. A. Packer.
Corpl. E. J. Pankhurst (Bar).
C.S.M. H. E. Patterson.
L/Sergt. A. Pattinson (Bar).
L/Corpl. W. E. Pearce.
L/Corpl. W. C. Peters.
Rfn. A. Post.
Corpl. E. J. Roberts.
Corpl. S. Roff.
Rfn. W. T. Rowe.
L/Sergt. F. Sando.
Sergt. W. H. Saunders.
Rfn. T. Schofield.
L/Corpl. W. Scott.
Rfn. J. F. Seager.
Rfn. E. W. Sharp.
L/Corpl. A. Sherwin.

APPENDIX II

L/Corpl. M. Sherwin.
Rfn. B. Skelton.
Corpl. J. Snape.
Rfn. R. Stacey (Bar).
C.S.M. C. H. Stenning, M.C.
Rfn. T. J. Stevens.
Sergt. J. W. Stott, D.C.M.
Sergt. H. C. Streeton.
Rfn. W. Thorndick.
Rfn. H. Thorpe.
Rfn. J. Tindell.
L/Sergt. F. H. Titley.
L/Corpl. G. W. Todd.
Rfn. M. Tombs.
Rfn. E. Travis.
L/Corpl. F. Trevett.
Rfn. A. R. Tribe.
Rfn. C. H. Trigg.
Rfn. J. Turner.
Rfn. W. E. Turner.
Corpl. J. E. Twinn.
Rfn. J. D. Vaughan.
Rfn. B. L. Vincent.
L/Corpl. C. Walker.
Corpl. W. Wall.
Rfn. G. W. Waller.
Rfn. J. D. Ward.
L/Sergt. H. Warner.
Rfn. T. Watts.
Rfn. G. Westcombe.
Rfn. G. White.
Rfn. P. White.
Rfn. V. White.
Rfn. S. Whiting.
Rfn. S. Wigg.
Rfn. B. Wildman.
Sergt. W. B. Wilkinson.
L/Sergt. I. Williams.
L/Cpl. A. Willson.
Rfn. J. Wilmot.
L/Corpl. E. A. Wilson.
Rfn. R. P. Withers.
Rfn. L. G. Wood.
Sergt. R. Wood.
Sergt. S. J. Woods.
Sergt. T. Woof.
Rfn. S. Worrilow.
L/Corpl. A. Wright.

THE MERITORIOUS SERVICE MEDAL

Rfn. W. J. Brooks.
Sergt. A. J. Classen.
C.S.M. T. B. Jolly.
C.S.M. J. Keene.
R.S.M. J. R. Miles.
Corpl. C. A. Remnant.
Sergt. S. E. Renton.
R.Q.M.S. D. W. L. Richards.
Sergt. D. H. Rowlands.

FOREIGN DECORATIONS
Croix de Guerre (French)
C.S.M. F. J. Oliver, M.C., M.M.

Medaille Militaire (French)
Corpl. W. Beesley, V.C.   Rfn. D. B. Field.

*Chevalier de l'Ordre de la Couronne avec
Croix de Guerre (Belgian)*
2nd Lieut. P. F. Davy, M.C.   Capt. E. W. Wood, M.C.
Corpl. F. Anthony, D.C.M.   Sergt. W. A. Balchin, D.C.M.

Bronze Medal for Military Valour (Italian)
Corpl. C. A. Johnson, M.M.

Medal of St. George, Second Class (Russian)
Sergt. E. Manktelow, D.C.M., M.M.

*   *   *

The names of the Officers and Men who were mentioned in Despatches have been omitted because it has not been possible to obtain a complete list.

APPENDIX III

The full story, as recorded in the "London Gazette," of the deeds for which the Victoria Cross was awarded.

Sergt. W. Gregg, D.C.M., M.M.

For most conspicuous bravery and brilliant leadership in action. Two Companies of his unit attacked the enemy's outpost position without artillery preparation. Sergt. Gregg was with the Right Company, which came under heavy fire from the right flank as it advanced. All the officers of the Company were hit. He at once took command of the attack. He rushed an enemy post and personally killed an entire machine-gun team, and captured the gun and four men in a dug-out near by. He then rushed another post, killed two men and captured another. In spite of heavy casualties he reached his objective and started consolidating the position. By this prompt and effective action this gallant Non-Commissioned officer saved the situation at a critical time and ensured the success of the attack. Later, Sergt. Gregg's party were driven back by an enemy counter-attack, but, reinforcements coming up, he led a charge, personally bombed a hostile machine-gun, killed the crew and captured the gun. Once again he was driven back. He led another successful attack, and hung on to the position until ordered by his Company Commander to withdraw. Although under very heavy rifle and machine-gun fire for several hours, Sergt. Gregg displayed throughout the greatest coolness and contempt of danger, walking about encouraging his men and setting a magnificent example.

Rfn. W. Beesley

For most conspicuous bravery. The enemy's outpost position was attacked by two Companies of his unit without artillery preparation. Rifleman Beesley was in the leading wave of the Left Company, which came under heavy fire as it approached the enemy's front line. His Platoon sergeant and all the section commanders were killed. This young soldier, realizing the situation, at once took command and led the assault. Single-handed he rushed a post, and with his revolver killed two of the enemy at a machine-gun. He then shot dead an officer who ran across from a dug-out to take their place at the machine-gun. Three more officers appeared from the dug-out. These he called on to surrender; seeing one of them trying to get rid of a map he shot him and obtained the map. He took four more prisoners from a dug-out and two others from a shelter close by, disarmed them and sent them back to our lines. At this moment his Lewis gun was brought up by a comrade, who was acting as a carrier. Rifleman Beesley at once brought it into action, and used it with great effect against the enemy as they bolted towards their Support lines, inflicting many casualties. For four hours Rifleman Beesley and his comrade held on to the position under very heavy machine-gun and rifle fire. The enemy then advanced to counter-attack, and the other soldier was wounded. Rifleman Beesley carried on by himself and actually maintained his position until 10 p.m., long after the posts on his right and left had been practically wiped out and the survivors had fallen back. It was mainly due to his action that the enemy were prevented from rushing the position, and that the remnants of his Company, when compelled to withdraw, were able to do so without further loss. When darkness set in Rifleman Beesley made his way back to the original line from which the attack had started, bringing with him the wounded carrier and the Lewis gun. He at once mounted the Lewis gun in the trench and remained in action until things quietened down. The indomitable pluck, skilful shooting, and good judgment in economizing ammunition displayed by Rifleman Beesley stamped the incident as one of the most brilliant actions in recent operations.

www.ingramcontent.com/pod-product-compliance
Lightning Source LLC
Chambersburg PA
CBHW040257170426
43192CB00020B/2832